Listen to Make Better Connections

A practical guide to reading people, asking deeper questions, staying present, building trust, and creating stronger conversations anywhere

George Munson

GL DIGITAL
PUBLISHING
LLC

Copyright © 2026 by George Munson

All rights reserved

No portion of this book may be reproduced without written permission from the publisher or author except as permitted by U.S. copyright law.

This publication is designed to provide accurate and authoritative information regarding the subject matter covered. It is sold with the understanding that neither the author nor the publisher is engaged in rendering legal, investment, accounting, or other professional services.

While the publisher and author have used their best efforts in preparing this book, they make no representations or warranties with respect to the accuracy or completeness of the contents of this book and specifically disclaim any implied warranties of merchantability or fitness for a particular purpose. No warranty may be created or extended by sales representatives or written sales materials.

The advice and strategies contained herein may not be suitable for your situation. You should consult with a professional when appropriate. Neither the publisher nor the author shall be liable for any loss of profit or other commercial damages, including but not limited to special, incidental, consequential, personal, or other damages.

Neither the publisher nor the author claims responsibility for the persistence or accuracy of URLs for external or third-party Internet Websites referred to in this publication, and does not guarantee that any content on such Websites is, or will remain, accurate or appropriate.

Designations used by companies to distinguish their products are often claimed as trademarks. All brand names and product names used in this book and on its cover are trade names, service marks, trademarks and registered trademarks of their respective owners. The publishers and the book are not associated with any product or vendor mentioned in this book. None of the companies referenced within the book have endorsed the book.

First Edition 2026

Contents

Introduction

Listening goes beyond just nodding or agreeing. When we stop really hearing each other, misunderstandings happen. This can lead to damaged projects, weaker relationships, lost trust, and regret that sticks around.

Most of us want better conversations and deeper connections. We want to be heard and understood, and to give others the same feeling. Recognizing that listening can boost your confidence in relationships makes you feel more capable of creating meaningful connections.

Just knowing that listening is important isn't enough. The real challenge is turning that knowledge into action, especially when life gets busy. Listening well doesn't happen automatically. It's hard, but it matters.

For most of us, listening isn't something that comes naturally. We're taught to speak up, share our ideas, and make ourselves heard. But who actually teaches us how to listen? Many people think good listeners are just born that way or pick it up easily. I've learned, sometimes the hard way, that listening is a skill you can practice and improve. When you do, relationships get stronger, conflicts get smaller, and trust grows, even though workplace disagreements can start to fade.

I haven't always been a good listener. Honestly, I started writing this book because I needed it too. I've missed signals and made mistakes. There have been times when I thought I was listening, but really, I was waiting for my turn to speak or planning my response. I know how easy it is to get it wrong, and how much better life feels when you get it right. My journey has had ups and downs, but every time I got better at listening, I noticed real changes at work, with friends, and at home.

Listening is a practical skill that anyone can learn. You don't need any special talent, just some tools, practice, and a willingness to try. As you practice, you'll feel a sense of achievement and motivation from seeing your progress in better connections and fewer frustrations.

This book stands out because it doesn't just talk about listening; it gives you real strategies you can use in every part of your life. You'll learn how to build empathy, spot and overcome barriers, and use nonverbal cues to help you. We'll explore listening in different cultures, online, and in those tough conversations everyone dreads. I'll share stories from my own life and from others who have learned to listen with intention. You'll also get practical exercises, quick checklists, and honest answers to questions you might have felt too awkward to ask.

Maybe you're skeptical. Maybe you've tried to be a better listener before, and it didn't last. Maybe you worry that people won't notice, or that it's too late to change old habits. If that sounds familiar, I understand. I've been there, too. But you can do this. This isn't about being perfect or never making mistakes. It's about making small, steady changes by showing up with curiosity and openness.

You might be thinking about your last conversation that didn't go well. Maybe it was a disagreement, a tough talk, or just a regular moment that felt off. That's actually a great place to begin. As you read, bring those moments with you. Be honest about what's working and what isn't. Notice your own habits when you lose focus, interrupt, or feel triggered. This book is here to guide you, but you're the one who shapes your journey.

Let's learn to listen in a way that can change everything. Whether you want to resolve conflict, lead, support others, or connect more deeply, this book can help. You're in the right place, so let's get started together.

Chapter One

Why Listening Changes Everything

Have you ever walked away from a conversation feeling unsettled or replaying it in your head? Maybe you thought you explained yourself, but your coworker got defensive, or your partner stopped talking. Sometimes, it feels like your words don't even register. These moments hurt and often stick with us. Many people don't realize how much is at risk when listening breaks down, relationships suffer, work becomes tense, and people feel misunderstood. We all want to be heard, but it's hard for many to listen in return.

Listening quietly connects us all. When we listen well, trust and teamwork grow, making the reader feel valued and capable of strengthening relationships. When we don't, things can fall apart. Poor listening doesn't just cause awkward moments or minor mix-ups; it leads to missed opportunities and broken trust, sometimes with consequences that are bigger than we expect. People often value speaking, but listening is what really shapes our relationships and choices. Yet, it's easy to overlook in our busy, distracted lives.

The Cost of Not Listening Often Leads to Misunderstandings, Missed Connections, and Lost Opportunities

Let's see what can go wrong when listening fails in serious situations. At work, for example, a manager might check their phone during a meeting and only half-listen to a team member's warning. If that warning becomes a real problem, it's not just about a failed project; trust fades, and people stop being open. Research from the Kenan Institute calls this "extractive listening," in which someone takes only what's useful right now, missing the bigger picture. This habit hurts teamwork and makes people feel like they don't really matter.

This happens at home as well. Imagine a parent doing several things at once while their child tries to talk about something important. Even if nothing is said, kids notice when their parents aren't really paying attention. Over time, they might stop sharing, thinking it's better to stay quiet than be ignored. This feeling can affect their relationships for years to come.

There are also less obvious listening problems at work. On video calls, you might believe you're listening, but distractions or thinking about your to-do list can make you miss important details. You might nod along but miss a client's main concern or a coworker's warning. These small mistakes can add up, leading to lost sales, failed projects, and team members who stop sharing because they don't feel heard.

Poor listening isn't always obvious. Sometimes, it's the small things, like finishing someone's sentence, guessing what they'll say next, or only half-listening while you plan your own response. These habits slowly break down trust. If you often hear, "I thought you meant...", it could mean you're making assumptions instead of really understanding. Recognizing these habits can empower you to improve, making you feel confident in your ability to connect better.

The emotional effects are real. Being ignored in meetings isn't just frustrating; it can make you want to stop sharing your ideas. I once watched a talented coworker stop speaking up after her ideas were dismissed early on. She eventually left for a place where she felt valued, and her old team lost out. The same thing happens in friendships; if someone is always interrupted, they stop opening up, and the relationship becomes shallow. Improving listening can help you build resilience and foster meaningful connections.

Each time we don't listen well, we miss a chance to connect more deeply. Over time, these moments add up: a great employee leaves, a creative idea goes unshared, a customer leaves after feeling ignored, or a marriage suffers from years of not really hearing each other.

Take a Moment ...

Think back over the last week. Was there a moment you felt misunderstood or overlooked? Or did someone else seem dissatisfied with your response? Take a moment to jot down what happened and how you felt, honestly and without self-criticism. These moments point directly to the power of better listening.

Every missed connection, whether it's ignoring a warning or cutting someone off, affects not just conversations but whole relationships and workplaces. Good listening helps avoid these problems and builds trust, sparks new ideas, and leads to real teamwork wherever you are.

Why "Just Stay Quiet" Isn't Enough

A common myth is that listening means letting someone talk. Many people think it's about staying quiet, nodding, and looking polite. But just sitting there while someone speaks isn't real listening; it can make the other person feel ignored or judged. For example, a partner who stays silent during an argument might think they're helping, but their silence can make things worse and leave the other person feeling dismissed. The same goes for a manager who doesn't ask questions or give feedback after a presentation; it can make it seem as if they don't care about what was shared.

Another mistake is thinking that nodding or saying things like "Right" or "I see" is enough. Many of us do this, smiling and pretending to pay attention while our minds wander. It's easy to fake engagement in groups or long meetings. But people can tell when we're not really present, and over time, this weakens trust and connection.

It's also common to think that listening means waiting for your turn to speak. You might stay quiet, but really, you're just planning what to say next instead of focusing on the other person. This isn't real listening; it's just waiting to talk. When you do this, you can miss what the other person is really saying or twist it to fit your own ideas. Jumping in with your thoughts too soon often shows that you didn't fully understand, which can hurt your relationships.

Just being silent can backfire, too. If a friend or partner tunes out during a tough conversation, arms crossed and eyes glazed over, things often get worse because it feels like nothing is getting through. Silence without real interest shuts down the connection. The same is true for managers who never ask questions or check if they understood; employees start to wonder if anyone cares about what they say.

Good listening isn't about sitting still. It's active and goes both ways. It means being curious and showing you're engaged with your words and body language. You might repeat what you heard, like, "Are you saying this deadline is unrealistic?" or ask questions to make sure you understand, such as, "Did I get that right?" Even small changes, like asking, "Can you tell me more about what's worrying you?" instead of just saying "Uh-huh," can change the whole conversation. Your facial expressions, posture, and timing matter, even on video calls; people can see if you're really paying attention.

If you've tried advice like "just listen more" and felt let down, you're not alone. Simply not interrupting doesn't always create real understanding. Most tips overlook real-life challenges, such as hidden feelings, cultural differences, or digital distractions. Real listening means picking up on meaning, responding thoughtfully, and making sure both people feel understood.

This book will offer more than the usual advice. You'll get practical tools you can use every day, like how to paraphrase, check your assumptions, and stay focused even when you're distracted. We'll look at why people sometimes feel ignored, even when things are quiet, and how being more engaged can fix that. You don't have to be perfect or super patient; what matters is being curious and willing to check in with others.

Try a Listening Quick Check

Take out your notes. Think of a recent conversation where you or someone else stayed quiet, but there wasn't a real connection. What signs showed that real listening wasn't happening? Write down three things you noticed. Then, write one thing you could do next time to show more curiosity, like asking a follow-up question or repeating what you heard before you respond. These small changes can turn silence into a real connection.

Listening as a Learnable Superpower, Science, Stories, and Hope

If you've ever thought, "I'm just not a natural listener," you're not alone. But research shows our brains can change and adapt. This ability, called neuroplasticity, means we can form new habits with practice, even as adults. Listening isn't something you're born with or not; it's a skill you can build over time. Studies back this up. Daniel Goleman, who studies emotional intelligence, says attention is like a muscle; you can train it to focus better, connect more deeply, and avoid distractions. Listening activates parts of the brain tied to empathy, memory, and social skills. When you practice listening, you're not just being polite; you're actually changing your brain to connect better with others.

Real change happens when people try new things in real life. For example, a team at a tech company used to have meetings where no one really listened, and people talked over each other. Then they started some new "listening rituals. According to a study by Osnat Bouskila-Yam and Nurit Zaidman, when team members viewed listening in meetings positively and felt their team leader listened well, they tended to speak for longer periods without interruption, and their team leaders interrupted less often. People felt safer sharing, meetings were shorter, and decisions came faster because everyone understood what was being discussed. Team members even said they trusted each other more. That's what happens when people listen on purpose.

I've seen personal relationships change, too. I know a couple who grew apart after years of not really listening to each other. They were both frustrated and didn't know how to fix it. They agreed that during tough talks, the listener would repeat back what they heard before responding. This wasn't therapy, just a simple tool they used at home or on walks. Over time, their arguments got less intense, and they started to reconnect. Small changes in how they listened led to big improvements in trust.

If you're unsure because you've tried before and slipped back into old habits, don't worry. Change doesn't have to be big to make a difference. Small steps lead to real results. For example, doing a quick "summary check" at the end of a conversation ("So what I'm hearing is...") can clear up confusion fast. Taking a short pause before you reply gives your brain time to process, rather than jumping in with old ideas. These small habits add up and build your confidence.

You might notice that great listeners often have more influence. There's a reason for this. In leadership, people talk about Satya Nadella or Jacinda Ardern as examples. These leaders don't take over conversations; they ask thoughtful questions, repeat what they hear, and make others feel noticed. Nadella changed Microsoft's culture by focusing on empathy and curiosity. Ardern's calm and attentive style helped her earn trust during tough times. Their influence isn't magic; it comes from choosing to listen first, every time.

Listening isn't just good for others; it helps you handle conflict, build strong connections, and notice problems before they get bigger. Researcher Julian Treasure explains that deep listening helps you see past the noise and find hidden opportunities. When people feel heard, they relax and share their best ideas.

There's real hope, even if you're used to "half-listening" or grew up in a family where people didn't pay much attention. You can learn to listen with purpose, and people will notice. Start small: put your phone away when talking, ask one clarifying question each day, and try summarizing before you respond. You'll see people open up more and trust you more.

Science shows that listening changes your brain, your relationships, and your results. The stories prove that anyone can get better, even if you feel distracted or impatient now. Even one or two small changes this week can make a big difference. Listening isn't just a bonus; it's a superpower for leading teams, building strong relationships, and making a real impact in every part of life.

Overcoming the "Why Bother?" When Listening Feels Pointless or Draining

You might ask, "Why bother listening?" Maybe you've tried before, with coworkers, family, or friends who vent, and felt like it didn't help. Sometimes, you listen, and no one notices, or the other person keeps talking and never changes. Listening can feel thankless, especially with people who dominate conversations or in places where kindness is seen as weakness. If you've dealt with toxic workplaces or constant complainers, it's normal to feel tired or discouraged. You might even think, "Some people just aren't worth it." That's a real feeling, especially if you've been let down before.

But even when listening feels pointless, it usually isn't. You don't need everyone to be a great communicator, your own effort can make a difference. Even imperfect listening changes the mood. Conflicts cool down, meetings feel less tense, and conversations at home get easier. Staying calm helps, even with difficult people. I've seen tense meetings improve when one person reflects what was said, and arguments at home get easier when someone pauses to understand. These aren't huge changes, but small moments add up. Meetings go better, misunderstandings happen less, and stress drops. You won't fix every relationship, but you'll notice more peace day to day.

With work, family, and constant notifications, listening can feel like just another task or something you'll never get right. But real listening doesn't require endless patience or much time. It works best in small moments, a five-minute check-in at a meeting or a pause before you react to your child. Short bursts of attention matter more than big gestures. For example, asking a real question after dinner can do more than an hour of distracted talking. Just a few focused minutes each day can make a big difference. In offices, I've seen teams go from chaos to clarity by letting everyone share their top concern for sixty seconds before meetings start. That's often enough to stop bigger problems.

Listening helps you, too. It's not just about helping others; it's also a form of self-care and a way of setting boundaries. When you listen on purpose, you can tell what's your responsibility and what isn't, notice signs of burnout in yourself and others, and stay present without taking on everyone's feelings. Think of listening as a way to manage stress and clear up confusion or resentment. Deciding when and how much to listen keeps you from feeling overwhelmed.

If you're tired from dealing with people who talk too much or situations that drain you, remember: listening doesn't mean you have to be available all the time or give up your needs. Sometimes, it means saying, "I care, but I need a break." Or choosing to really listen for five minutes instead of half-listening for an hour. Setting boundaries is healthy, not selfish. Being present doesn't mean letting others walk all over you.

If you're busy and rarely have quiet time, remember: the goal is progress, not perfection. Small moments count. One real question is better than twenty minutes of distracted nodding. Listening helps you, too; you'll feel less stressed, sleep better, and carry less tension. Even if others don't change, your own experience will improve.

Listening isn't a huge sacrifice; it's a simple way to make space for yourself and build real connections. It won't fix every problem or make everyone happy, but it helps life feel less dramatic and more genuine. Even when it seems like no one notices, it's still worth doing.

The Ripple Effect, or How Using Better Listening Skills Elevates Teams, Families, and Communities

Imagine a workplace where people share ideas without worrying about being judged or ignored. There's a special energy, team members look at each other, show real interest, and aren't afraid to take risks. This kind of atmosphere doesn't just happen; it grows when people feel safe, and that safety comes from regular, attentive listening. Researchers call this "psychological safety," and it's one of the best signs that a team will be creative instead of stuck. When leaders and coworkers really listen, questions are welcome, mistakes become learning moments, and creative ideas come forward. A Google study found that psychological safety, built mostly through active listening, sets their best teams apart.

One person's commitment to listening differently can change a group's culture faster than you might think. Imagine someone consistently "signal boosting" others, repeating and highlighting a colleague's idea in a meeting so it's not lost in the shuffle. Before long, others notice and start doing the same. In families, this spreads in small but meaningful ways. Maybe you begin reflecting on what your teen says at dinner instead of rushing to advice or judgment. Your spouse picks up on it and tries it next time there's a disagreement. Soon, even the youngest members chime in with their own versions, and the family dinner table starts to feel less like a battleground and more like a place where people genuinely want to understand one another.

The measurable outcomes of better listening ripple out further than most people expect. In companies where leaders introduce structured listening practices, such as regular feedback loops or check-ins, employee retention often increases. People stay where they feel heard. Engagement scores rise, not because of elaborate perks but because people trust their voices matter. Teams solve problems faster because no one hoards information or hides a concern out of fear. Feedback becomes more accurate and less personal, which means less drama and more growth.

Outside the office, stronger listening habits bolster relationships in ways that last. Couples who adopt weekly "listening sessions", short windows in which one person speaks while the other listens without interruption, report fewer misunderstandings and more intimacy over time. Friends who make space for each other's stories grow more resilient against life's stressors because they know support is steady and real. Even neighborhoods feel the difference: community groups that welcome every voice, especially quieter ones, see higher participation and less conflict around local decisions.

You can spot these shifts in subtle "before and after" snapshots. At one company, team meetings used to be tense, with only the boldest speaking up while others hung back. After a few months of intentional listening rituals, like summarizing what was said before moving on, attendance improved, ideas flowed more freely, and even introverted employees contributed insights that shaped big projects. In families adopting structured listening practices (like "talking stick" rules or weekly check-ins), kids started bringing up challenges earlier, rather than bottling up their feelings until they exploded. Marriages once colored by sarcasm or avoidance warmed into places where partners felt safe disagreeing, knowing they'd both get heard.

Communities benefit too. When town hall facilitators model active listening, paraphrasing concerns, and asking clarifying questions, the tone shifts from adversarial to collaborative. Residents stay longer, participate more, and often reach agreements that felt impossible before.

Now imagine if only ten percent more people in your circle started listening as they meant it. What might change? You'd see fewer misunderstandings and more honest feedback at work. Family gatherings would be filled with laughter rather than tension. Community groups would move forward with less friction and more shared purpose. Even random daily encounters at the coffee shop or in line at the grocery store would feel lighter, as people sense genuine attention rather than blank stares or hurried glances.

The beauty is that these changes don't require sweeping reforms or endless training sessions. It starts with one person deciding to show up differently, to listen fully, respond thoughtfully, and signal that every voice matters. Others notice and often follow suit, creating a wave of positive change that grows wider than you might expect.

Listening isn't just about improving individual relationships; it rewires the DNA of entire groups for resilience, creativity, and connection. When listening spreads, even a little, the impact multiplies in ways that last far beyond a single conversation. And that is how real transformation begins: one attentive ear at a time.

Chapter Two

Diagnosing Your Listening Blind Spots

Micro-Moments of Miscommunication, Spotting Your Hidden Patterns

Imagine walking from your desk to the kitchen at work, coffee mug in hand, when a colleague stops you for a quick update. You might catch just enough to nod along, but later, someone is confused, or a task gets missed. It's not a crisis yet. These small moments, those quick exchanges between meetings and decisions, are where most miscommunication starts. Misunderstandings rarely appear out of nowhere. They usually build up in these brief interactions, like check-ins by the copier or a quick "Can you talk for a sec?" message. One missed detail or cue, and suddenly you're facing problems you didn't expect.

We tend to remember the big arguments or emails that get out of hand, but it's the small mistakes that slowly weaken our connections. You might hear someone ask, "Did you hear what I just said?" and realize you weren't really listening. Or you might say, "That's not what I meant," after someone reacts in a way you didn't expect. These phrases are warning signs that something got lost between what was said and what was understood. They show up everywhere: at dinner, on Slack, in doctors' offices, or even while talking with friends at the gym.

Many people miss these signs because they expect miscommunication to be obvious and dramatic. In reality, it often slips in quietly, a moment when you misread someone's tone or forget to ask a follow-up question. Maybe it happens as you rush out the door and your partner tries to share something important, or during a meeting when a teammate's idea goes unnoticed. These small lapses might seem minor, but over time, they add up. When someone says, "You never listen," it's usually about many small moments that made them feel ignored.

The key is to notice your own patterns. Everyone has certain situations where communication breaks down, such as when you're on your phone or multitasking. Paying attention to when and where these moments happen helps you spot your blind spots before they cause bigger problems. For example, if you often hear, "Are you even listening?" during these times, that's a sign to focus more intentionally.

A Three-Day Listening Diary as Your Self-Discovery Tool

A simple way to notice these habits is to keep a three-day listening diary. For the next three days, write down notes after your conversations, especially if you felt uneasy or unsure. Don't worry about grammar, just record when you feel misunderstood, missed something, or need to clarify later. Watch for phrases like "That's not what I meant" or "Can you repeat that?" Note how often they come up and what was happening at the time. You'll start to see patterns, such as certain topics or group settings where these moments occur.

When you look over your diary, ask yourself where misunderstandings happen most and what actions you can take. Are there specific people or situations that seem to cause them? For instance, if your spouse feels ignored in the evenings, plan to give them your full attention then. The real value of this exercise is not just spotting mistakes but using these insights to intentionally improve your communication.

These small moments matter more than we realize. In relationships, repeated small lapses can slowly erode trust. If a spouse hears "Hold on, I'm busy" too often, they might stop sharing. A friend who feels left out during group gatherings may start to pull away. Over time, excitement fades, work meetings become routine, and family conversations lose depth. It's not one big event that causes this, but the ongoing feeling of being brushed off that weakens the connection.

Noticing these subtle patterns lets you address them before they become bigger issues. When you realize you're in a familiar situation, like tuning out during a routine update, you can pause and make a different choice. Maybe you ask one more question or repeat what you heard to be sure. These small changes may seem simple, but they make a big difference over time.

It's like taking care of a garden. If you ignore weeds, they don't go away; they just spread. Noticing and naming your small moments of miscommunication is the first step to clearing them out so a real connection can grow.

The Zone-Out Trap, Recognizing When You've Checked Out

You've probably had that awkward moment when someone asks, "Wait, what did I just say?" and you can't remember their last words. That's the zone-out trap, when you're there in person, but your mind is somewhere else. Maybe you nod and say "yeah, totally," but you're really thinking about an email or dinner plans. Your eyes might glaze over, you might yawn and try to hide it, or on Zoom, you might pretend to take notes while looking at other tabs. Zoning out can happen quickly; one moment you're paying attention, the next you're not.

Why do we zone out? Stress is a big reason. When you're overwhelmed by deadlines or personal issues, your mind looks for a break. Boredom can also cause it; if a conversation feels slow or repetitive, you might go on autopilot. Digital distractions make it even harder. A phone ping, a notification, or the urge to multitask can all pull your focus away. When you think you're multitasking, like listening and emailing, your brain is just switching quickly between tasks, not fully paying attention to either. This is even easier to hide in virtual meetings, especially when the camera is off and the sound is muted.

The signs that you've zoned out include your eyes glazing over or darting around, slow nodding, or saying "uh-huh" or "right" without real engagement. You might find yourself rereading the same line in a document or forgetting details soon after, which shows you weren't truly present. Recognizing these cues helps you re-engage in the moment and improve your listening habits.

How can you catch yourself before zoning out becomes a problem? Try a mental reset. During a conversation, ask yourself, "Where is my attention right now?" Notice if you're thinking ahead or planning your response instead of listening. Pay attention to your body, tense shoulders, fidgeting with your phone, or tapping a pen can be signs you're distracted. If you notice you're drifting, gently bring your focus back by picking one thing about the speaker, like their expression, hand movements, or the sound of their voice.

Try this quick exercise: focus on one detail about how the person is speaking. Maybe their tone sounds tired, or their eyebrows are raised. Notice it to yourself, like thinking, "Her voice is softer than usual." This helps bring you back to the present. You can also ground yourself by noticing how your chair feels, the temperature in the room, or by taking a slow, deep breath as you listen.

Set up attention checkpoints during long meetings or conversations. Every ten minutes, or whenever you notice your focus slipping, pause and check in with yourself. Are you still paying attention? If not, ask a clarifying question or repeat what you've heard. This not only shows you care, but also helps you refocus.

Digital life makes deep listening harder. Notifications are meant to grab your attention. Before important calls or meetings, silence your phone, close any extra tabs, and put it away. Even these small steps can help you focus much better than you might think.

Everyone zones out sometimes, but it doesn't have to ruin your conversations. Being aware is a big part of the solution. The more you notice when you're drifting and bring your focus back, the easier it gets. Not every conversation will be exciting, but showing up and paying attention, even if you're not perfect, builds trust and shows respect that lasts.

Try to make it a habit to ask yourself, when you notice your focus slipping, "What's one thing I notice about this person right now?" You don't need to be perfect or always alert; keep returning to what matters: being present for people, even for a few minutes. That's how real understanding and meaningful conversations happen.

Interrupting, Advice-Giving, and "Fixer" Habits, Owning Your Go-To Responses

You probably know the urge: someone starts explaining a problem, and before they've finished, you're already preparing your reply or solution. You might even cut them off mid-sentence, thinking it will save time or help them out. This "fixer" reflex can feel helpful, but often leaves others feeling dismissed or unheard. A simple, "Have you tried...?" can suddenly shift a conversation from connection to correction, sometimes before it really begins.

These habits often stem from impatience; maybe you're in a hurry, think quickly, or feel uncomfortable when others are upset and want to ease their pain fast. Sometimes, you genuinely want to help or protect someone from struggling. But there's a downside: jumping in with solutions can signal that you value efficiency over empathy, or that you want to be right rather than truly hearing the issue. Over time, people might stop opening up, feeling it's safer to keep their thoughts to themselves.

Owning these habits starts with naming them. In conversations, notice when your mind races ahead or when you feel the urge to interject. Are you tensing up or holding your breath? Rehearsing your advice before the other person finishes? These are cues that your "fixer" mode is activating. Sometimes, advice is disguised as a question, "Have you thought about...?", which is really a setup to share your solution. Other times, it's a direct interruption or a sigh of impatience.

If this sounds familiar, don't be hard on yourself. Many of us grew up in environments where quick answers were rewarded, and silence felt awkward. But change starts by pausing and observing in real time. Next time someone shares a struggle, and you feel the urge to jump in, ask yourself: "What if I just waited 10 more seconds?" That discomfort means you're growing. You don't have to fill every silence; sometimes, just holding space is the most generous response.

A practical trick: before saying anything, count to three in your head. While waiting, focus on the other person's words, let them finish. If your mind floods with suggestions, imagine setting them aside for later. This restraint may feel odd, but it lets the speaker feel heard.

If you're about to offer advice or interrupt, try shifting your response. Instead of "You should..." or "Here's what I'd do," reflect what you've heard ("It sounds like work has been overwhelming") or ask an open question ("How do you feel about that?"). This encourages deeper conversation and shows you value their perspective. Often, people find their own answers when given enough space.

For example:

- **Your friend**: "I just don't know how to talk to my boss about this project."

- **Typical fixer**: "Have you tried emailing her first?"

- **Better response**: "What worries you most about that conversation?" or "Tell me more about what's on your mind."

Even if silence feels uneasy, remember not every pause needs filling. Presence without pressure, just being there as someone thinks out loud, can be powerful.

You can also try paraphrasing. After someone shares, repeat what you heard in your own words: "So you're saying this has been bothering you for a while?" This shows you're listening and clears up misunderstandings early.

Reflect after your next conversation: Did I interrupt? Did I advise being asked? What would have happened if I'd paused? Write down what felt different. These observations help shift your habits over time and create space for real listening, not just quick fixes.

Breaking these patterns isn't about suppressing your instincts or not caring; it's about choosing depth and connection over speed. The more you practice waiting or asking one more question before offering solutions, the easier it is for others to share openly with you. People don't always need answers; they need acknowledgment and a chance to be heard on their terms.

Identifying Emotional Triggers that Knock You Off Track

Everyone has conversations where, suddenly, your chest tightens, or your face heats up. Maybe it's your boss's feedback tone or a phrase that echoes a childhood scolding. These "listening triggers"- words, tones, gestures, or topics- snap you from openness straight into fight-or-flight mode. Sometimes you're conscious of it, jaw clenching, knee bouncing. Other times, you only realize after you're already defending yourself or shutting down. It's surprising how quickly you can switch from curious to guarded.

Triggers surface in feedback sessions, heated debates, and even casual chats when something taps an old wound. Maybe "Calm down" spikes your heart rate, or "We need to talk" makes you brace for the worst. These reactions usually stem from past experiences, years of family squabbles, a hypercritical teacher, or stressful evaluations. Your brain stores those moments, and when it encounters something similar, it automatically reacts as if the situation were the same.

Mapping your triggers is transformative. Reflect on recent conversations that made you defensive or angry. Was it specific words, someone's tone, their look, or the topic? Write down what stands out. For example, feedback like "I expected more from you" can set me off, even if there's no malice behind it. Family dynamics can also bring back old habits; maybe your sibling always interrupts, and you revert to sibling rivalry patterns. These situations help you spot what rattles you. Once you've listed them, notice if similar triggers appear in other scenarios, work meetings, group messages, or even texts.

When triggered, your focus narrows. You may stop hearing the other person and start replaying old arguments in your head. Defensive listening takes over, you interrupt to defend yourself, or rush to correct the record. Or, you disengage, nodding along while mentally checking out. In any case, the conversation derails. At this point, you're no longer listening to understand; you're listening to defend or escape, often before you're fully aware of it.

The goal is to identify these moments as they happen, not just in hindsight. If you notice your pulse rising or your shoulders tensing, recognize it as a warning from your body. Simply naming it to yourself, "I notice I'm getting defensive", provides enough distance for you to make a conscious choice before reacting.

A helpful tactic is pausing. If you sense a trigger, avoid responding immediately. Breathe in through your nose, out through your mouth, and let the pause last a bit longer than feels natural. This gives your emotions a moment to settle and your mind a second to catch up. You might even say, "I need a second to think about that." This isn't avoidance, but a way to preserve the quality of the conversation.

Setting boundaries in advance can help too. If certain topics always derail you, such as money discussions with a partner, job performance reviews, plan for them. Let others know what helps: "Could I get a heads-up before we talk about finances?" or "Can we check in halfway through so I can process?" Boundaries aren't about avoidance; they're about creating conditions for genuine listening.

Simple breathwork is also effective for calming your nerves. Try box breathing: inhale for 4 seconds, hold, exhale for 4 seconds, hold again for 4 seconds, and repeat while listening. This keeps you present and prevents spiraling thoughts.

Some triggers are sneaky and only become apparent in hindsight. If you look back and realize you got stuck on a specific word or tone, note it for next time. Over time, these patterns become easier to spot and easier to manage.

No one eliminates triggers; they're part of being human. But greater awareness of what disrupts your listening helps you recover more quickly and return to genuine engagement. Notice your reactions without judgment; treat them as valuable data. With practice, you'll build tools to keep yourself grounded and present, even when conversations get tense.

Self-Assessment Lab, Quizzes, and Prompts for Your Listening Profile

If you've ever wondered how your listening habits measure up, you're not alone. Most of us depend on gut feelings or occasional feedback, but a more structured self-assessment, a "listening lab", offers practical insights. Viewing listening as a skill to explore, not judge, helps you spot your patterns and make real changes. Here's where a practical quiz comes in: a 15-question survey covering all kinds of listening scenarios, from high-pressure discussions to distracted moments. The aim isn't to pass or fail, but to observe your habits.

Think of this quiz as a quick, honest mirror. It asks: How often do you lose track of what's said? Do you jump in with solutions too soon? How do you react with talkative colleagues, upset loved ones, or when you're tired? You'll spot patterns, maybe you're more attentive at work, or perhaps you get defensive with authority. Remember, this is only a snapshot, not a final verdict.

After finishing, review where your biggest challenges and strengths lie. Are you easily distracted, prone to interrupting, or struggle with managing emotions? Understanding these drivers is the first step to change. And don't gloss over your strengths; perhaps you're patient, or notice subtle cues others miss. These are assets to leverage.

Reflection deepens your insight. Grab a notebook and try prompts like: "When am I most present in conversation? What makes me tune out?" Consider different settings: At work, do you listen best in meetings or informal chats? At home, does your patience run thin at certain times or with certain topics? With friends, does face-to-face feel easier than texting? These questions reveal both pitfalls and shining moments so that you can replicate the latter.

Another valuable angle: ask for outside feedback. This can feel daunting, but it is invaluable. Choose one or two trusted individuals, maybe a partner or colleague, and ask, "Can you share one thing I do well as a listener, and one thing I could improve?" Or use a simple script:
"Hey! I'm working on becoming a better listener. Are there times when you feel especially heard by me, or times when I seem distracted? Any honest feedback would help me grow."

People might mention strengths, like your good eye contact, or habits to address, like checking your phone. Your job is to listen, thank them, and reflect; there's no need to defend or explain.

To keep things organized, create a personal "Listening Profile." Summarize the key points from your quiz and feedback: your top strengths, recurring challenges, and the situations where you listen best (or struggle most). This becomes your growth roadmap. If you prefer something tangible, use the provided worksheet to track observations and progress after important conversations.

Understanding your listening profile isn't about finding flaws; it's about building self-awareness and giving yourself a foundation for growth. When you see your patterns clearly, goal-setting becomes easier. For example, next week you might focus on avoiding interruptions in meetings or being more present during evening chats at home. These changes don't require giant leaps; small, steady steps add up fast.

In short, knowing yourself as a listener underpins every other skill in this book. With this honest self-portrait, shaped by your reflection and trusted feedback, you're set to try new tools with confidence. Self-awareness is always the beginning of growth.

As you wrap up this chapter, remember that blind spots aren't permanent. Now that you hold your listening profile, you're ready to learn the practical skills that turn self-knowledge into action. In the next chapter, we'll dive into active listening so that every conversation can become a genuine connection.

Chapter Three

Active Listening in Action

The Anatomy of an Active Listener is What Sets Them Apart

Imagine you're at a neighbor's barbecue, holding a plate of food and talking about work stress. One friend glances over now and then, keeps checking their phone, and hardly makes eye contact. The other friend puts their plate down, faces you, and responds with small prompts like "Oh, really?" and "Go on," giving you their full attention. You can feel the difference right away. One friend is distracted, while the other is really listening. That's the difference between passive and active listening.

Active listeners use their whole selves, starting with body language. They face you, keep their shoulders relaxed, arms uncrossed, and sit with an open posture. Leaning in a little shows genuine interest, helping you feel truly valued and understood. Their eyes stay on you, not on phones or other distractions. Sometimes, they naturally mirror your expressions or gestures, which helps build trust and shows empathy, making you feel noticed.

They show they're paying attention by using short, genuine phrases like "I see," "Right," or "Tell me more." These prompts are used thoughtfully, not just out of habit, and encourage you to keep sharing your story. Sometimes, just staying silent with an interested posture and expression is powerful too, making it easier for you to open up without feeling rushed. This approach helps you feel safe and supported in the conversation.

These actions come from a certain mindset. Active listeners are curious and try not to jump in to fix things, compete, or make a point. Instead of thinking about what to say next, they focus on really understanding the other person's words and feelings. I call this "listener's humility", being open to learning from every conversation, even if you think you know what's coming. It means setting aside your own thoughts to make room for someone else's experience. This mindset encourages you to feel more confident and open during conversations.

Active listeners also hold back from judging. Instead of seeing everything from their own point of view or making quick assumptions, they stay open, patient, and empathetic. They don't rush to fix or correct things; they let the other person finish and express themselves. This creates a safe space where people can be honest and open, something passive listeners often miss.

Consider two scenarios. In a tense team meeting, the passive manager folds their arms, checks emails, and gives distracted, generic responses. The engaged manager closes their laptop, leans forward, maintains eye contact, nods, and gently encourages reluctant speakers. They respond calmly when emotions rise, helping the team regain focus.

Or at home, the distracted parent scrolls through emails while their child talks about school, missing the child's point entirely. The attentive parent puts their device away, makes eye contact, and listens with encouraging nods and patient silence, prompting deeper conversation. The child feels validated and safe to share more openly.

Your Listening Vital Signs

Next time you're in a conversation, anywhere, do a quick scan for these "vital signs":

- **Posture:** Are you facing the person? Is your body relaxed and open?

- **Eye Contact:** Do you focus on the speaker, or are you pulled to other distractions?

- **Facial Expression:** Does your face show interest and encouragement? Are you nodding or smiling in sync with their mood?

If something doesn't feel right, make a small adjustment. Even little changes can have a big impact on how others feel your presence.

Active listening isn't about being perfect; it's about being present and intentional. The real difference between passive and active listeners comes from practice, not natural ability, and from how you use your body language, voice, and mindset. When you bring curiosity, humility, and open body language to a conversation, you help honesty and connection grow.

Paraphrase Back to Confirm Understanding Without Sounding Robotic

During difficult conversations, like when a coworker talks about a deadline or a friend shares a problem, you want to show you understand. But saying things like "What I hear you saying is..." can sound forced. Good paraphrasing helps people feel truly understood, not just listened to. It means reflecting the main message, especially when emotions are high or things aren't clear.

Paraphrasing acts as a safety net, catching miscommunications before they turn into bigger issues. If someone says, "I just feel like nobody listens in these meetings," you might respond, "You're frustrated because you feel your input gets ignored?" This approach can de-escalate tension and foster real dialogue, helping prevent minor misunderstandings from growing into resentment.

But if you use the same phrases like "So what I'm hearing is…" too often, you might sound distant or even patronizing. Repeating these lines can make your words feel less genuine and might make the other person feel like they're in a therapy session instead of having a real conversation. When emotions run high or topics are sensitive, adjust your tone and paraphrasing to be gentle and empathetic, such as, "It sounds like you're feeling overwhelmed," or "Let me see if I understand what you're experiencing." This helps create a safe space for honest dialogue.

In the workplace, if a colleague says, "I'm worried this deadline isn't realistic for our team," don't offer advice or dismiss their concern immediately. Instead, try, "You think we might be rushing things, and you're concerned about burnout?" This invites clarification without judgment. Or if a friend sighs, "I just can't seem to catch a break lately," you might reply, "Sounds like it's been one thing after another, and it's wearing you out." These responses show you're attentive to both their words and their emotions.

Here's a simple before-and-after example:

Before:
Colleague: "I'm overwhelmed with these tasks."
You: "Well, just let me know if you need help."

After:
Colleague: "I'm overwhelmed with these tasks."
You: "It sounds like your plate's way too full right now."

The second response shows that you recognize their stress, making it easier for them to open up honestly.

Or with a friend:

Before:
Friend: "I feel like nobody notices how hard I'm trying."
You: "You shouldn't think that way."

After:
Friend: "I feel like nobody notices how hard I'm trying."
You: "You're putting in so much effort, but it feels invisible."

Good paraphrasing isn't just about repeating words; it's about picking up on feelings and meaning. If you get it wrong and the other person corrects you, don't get defensive. Instead, thank them and show interest: "Thanks for clarifying, can you tell me more?" This shows you want to understand, not just be right.

It's normal for paraphrasing to feel awkward at first. You might worry about sounding fake or making mistakes. If that happens, just be honest: "I want to make sure I'm getting this, let me try to put it in my own words." If someone says you're off ("No, that's not what I meant"), stay curious instead of taking it personally: "Okay, help me get closer. What am I missing?" This way, even awkward moments can lead to better understanding.

To get more comfortable, practice paraphrasing in low-stakes situations: after meetings ("Just to check, are we all on the same page that our next step is X?") or in family conversations ("So you want Friday night to be just us at home?"). The more you practice, the more natural it becomes, even when conversations get tough.

Paraphrasing isn't about sounding smart or perfect. It's about helping people understand each other, catching misunderstandings early, and showing you care about what the other person is saying. This is how trust grows, and real conversations happen.

Clarifying Questions, Digging Deeper Without Interrogating

When you want to really understand someone, whether it's a frustrated coworker or a quiet teenager, how you ask questions is important. Clarifying questions aren't meant to put someone on the spot; they're gentle ways to say, "Help me understand you." These questions are guided by curiosity, not by trying to control the conversation.

It's easy to start asking probing questions, especially if you want to solve a problem or need more details. But questions like "Why did you..." or "How come you didn't..." can sound accusing and make people defensive. Clarifying questions, on the other hand, are open and invite people to share more. For example, instead of "Why are you upset?" you could ask, "Can you tell me what's been bothering you?" The first feels like a challenge, while the second feels like an invitation.

The best clarifying questions are simple, like "Can you say more about that?" "What were you thinking when that happened?" or "How did that make you feel?" In meetings, you might ask, "What part of this project do you find most challenging?" At home, "What was the hardest part of your day?" can help someone share real feelings. Even saying, "I'm not sure I follow, can you walk me through your thinking?" shows you want to understand.

You can ask specific questions without sounding stiff. For example, if someone says, "My efforts aren't noticed," you could ask, "Are there certain times when you feel that way?" This shows respect for their experience without making it feel like an interrogation. Using a friendly tone, open body language, relaxed posture, gentle eye contact, and a nod now and then also helps.

Clarifying in Action

Consider a manager receiving feedback from Sam:

> **Sam**: "I've been struggling with getting timely responses from other departments."
> **You**: "That sounds frustrating. Can you say more about when this happens?"
> **Sam**: "Usually around month-end when I need approvals."
> **You**: "So those delays mostly hit during crunch time. What impact does that have on your work?"
> **Sam**: "It puts me behind and makes my team scramble at the last minute."

Each question follows from what Sam just said, giving him space to explain more. There's no hurry to fix the problem; there's just time for him to share his thoughts.

Contrast this with an interrogative approach:

> **Manager**: "Why aren't you getting responses? Have you tried emailing more people? Who's holding things up? Did you escalate this?"
> **Sam**: (shrinking back) "I... uh... I could follow up more."

In this situation, Sam may feel put on the spot and stop sharing, feeling judged rather than listened to.

Everyday Examples

This can happen at home as well. If your partner comes home upset, try not to ask, "What happened? Who upset you? Did you say anything back?" Instead, use a softer approach like, "You seem off, do you want to talk about it?" If they start to share, you can ask, "What part of today stood out to you most?" This helps them talk about what matters without feeling questioned.

Pacing, Tone, and Empathy

The most important part of clarifying questions is your pacing and tone. Asking too many questions or sounding doubtful can make someone stop talking. Look for signs like short answers, crossed arms, or comments like "It's not a big deal." These are clues to slow down and listen more.

Balance your questions with empathy. Say things like, "That sounds stressful," or "I can see why that would be tough." This helps keep the conversation open and safe.

Keep It Simple and Sincere

If you're not sure what to ask, try saying, "I want to make sure I understand. Can you give an example?" or "I'm still figuring this out. Could we talk it through a bit more?" You don't need special words, just a real interest in understanding.

Clarifying questions help conversations go deeper than small talk and build real connections. If you use them patiently and kindly, even people who are usually reserved may start to open up.

How to Avoid Interrupting When You're Eager With the Power Pause

You probably know the urge to jump in, finish someone's sentence, or react before they're done talking. Maybe you're excited, think you already understand, or feel nervous about a pause. Most of us interrupt not to be rude, but because we're eager to join in. Still, these quick interruptions add up and can make others feel ignored or shut down. That's why the "power pause", waiting three seconds after someone finishes before you respond, can make a big difference.

The power pause is like a small mental break. You don't have to stop everything or make it awkward. It's just a moment to check if the other person is really done or just pausing to think. When you make this a habit, conversations slow down, and you notice more details, such as changes in someone's voice or facial expressions. Most importantly, you show that what they say matters.

Picture a tense conversation where someone shares bad news, like a friend saying they're struggling at work. You might want to jump in with comfort or advice right away. But if you use the power pause, you wait a moment and let their words sink in. This gives them space to keep talking, and they might share even more, like, "Honestly, I'm just scared I'll lose my job." Without that pause, they might not have said it.

This habit works in all kinds of conversations, not just serious ones. For example, in a team brainstorming session, if the quietest person finally speaks up, don't rush to respond or move on. Wait three seconds and let their words settle. Often, they'll add more, or someone else will build on their idea because there was space for it. That short pause can change the whole meeting.

You can add the power pause to your daily routine with simple reminders. Put a note on your laptop that says "Count to 3" before you speak in meetings or on calls. If you tend to answer quickly at home, take a slow breath before you reply. Even in complicated situations, you can pause by sipping water or writing a quick note before responding.

Here's how this can change real conversations. In a virtual meeting where people talk over each other, you might jump in as soon as someone finishes, so your point is heard, but theirs is lost. According to the Activist Handbook, pausing after a comment allows everyone to process and reflect on what was said, reducing confusion, giving quieter people time to finish their thoughts, and encouraging thoughtful participation.

In another example, if your partner shares something personal after dinner, don't jump in with advice or your own story right away. Instead, finish chewing, take a breath, and wait a moment before responding. This pause might feel strange at first, but it often encourages them to share more or explain what they need from you, whether it's support, feedback, or just someone to listen.

Building this habit takes practice. Start by noticing when you want to interrupt, maybe you lean forward or open your mouth before the other person is done. When you feel that urge, try holding your hands together or silently counting to three in your head. You might find yourself relaxing as you focus on really listening.

Try this simple exercise: pick one conversation each day to practice the power pause after every time someone speaks. If you sometimes forget, that's okay, even a pause is progress. With practice, it will feel natural, and people will open up more because they know you're really listening rather than just waiting to respond.

You'll notice that conversations feel less rushed and more rewarding for everyone. You might even learn things you would have missed if you spoke too soon. The power pause is not only about remaining silent but also about showing respect for others' perspectives and allowing yourself time to fully grasp what others are communicating, which can support better team performance, as highlighted in a review by Krenz and Burtscher.

Signal boosting is a straightforward yet impactful approach to improving group conversations, wherever they occur, by ensuring that everyone's voice is heard and valued. It means making sure someone else's idea, question, or concern gets noticed. This is especially important for people who are quieter, new, or often overlooked. Sometimes, a good point is ignored until someone louder repeats it. Signal boosting stops this by highlighting contributions right when they happen.

In a meeting, signal boosting can be as simple as saying, "I want to revisit what Maria just said because we need to consider." This gives her idea another chance and shows the group that everyone's voice matters. It creates respect, and when people see that their input is valued, they're more likely to share again. Signal boosting isn't about overpraising; it's about fairness and making sure good ideas aren't missed.

You can use signal boosting in groups in simple but effective ways. In a virtual meeting, if someone's chat comment is missed, you could say, "I want to echo what Jamal mentioned earlier. I think it's worth discussing." At home, if your child is interrupted, you might say, "Alex, you started to say something before, do you want to finish your thought?" These small actions help everyone feel included and encourage open conversation.

Real-Life Impact

For example, I worked with a team where Rachel had great ideas but didn't speak up much and was often overlooked. We started making a point of repeating or giving credit to quieter voices. In one meeting, Rachel suggested a solution for a tech problem. A colleague said, "I want to highlight Rachel's workaround. Can we discuss it?" The team listened, discussed her idea, and ultimately used it. Recognizing Rachel boosted morale, and soon others started doing the same, making meetings more productive.

This also happens in text-based settings. On Slack or Teams, someone's good idea can be missed. Saying something like, "Echoing what Priya mentioned above, I think her idea about onboarding could really help," can bring the conversation back and show her input matters. The same holds in family group chats or community groups; signal-boosting helps keep things fair and balanced.

How to Start

If you're new to signal boosting, try these prompts:

In meetings: "Before we move on, I'd love to circle back to what Sam said earlier."

In group chats: "Echoing what Lee shared above, really important point."

At the dinner table: "Let's pause a second; Maya had something to say."

In brainstorming: "Can we spend another minute on Jordan's suggestion?"

Signal boosting can also help address power imbalances and reduce conflict. If certain people are consistently interrupted, make it your mission to ensure their voices are heard. Sometimes, simply saying, "I noticed we haven't heard from Amina yet. Amina, do you want to weigh in?" can shift the whole group's energy.

Signal boosting is not about awkwardly calling people out; it's about using your voice to support others when needed. The more you do it, the easier and more natural it becomes, and people will remember that you made space for them.

Wrapping Up

In summary, what sets great listeners apart is not just paying attention, but creating space for others to be heard and valued. Whether you're paraphrasing, asking clarifying questions, pausing before replying, or amplifying others' voices, these habits improve any conversation. Up next, we'll dig into what can get in the way of these good intentions and how you can break down those barriers before they trip you up.

Chapter Four

Empathy Without Overload

Empathy Muscle Training, Practical Ways to Build Compassion

Think about those times when you scroll past an online argument or go through the grocery store without really connecting with anyone. Many people believe empathy is something you're born with, like having curly hair or being left-handed. But actually, empathy works more like a muscle than a fixed trait. According to an article by Jonathan Levy and Oren Bader, empathy can be thought of as something that develops and strengthens through regular use, much like exercising a muscle that benefits from consistent attention, care, and rest. You wouldn't try to lift 200 pounds if you'd never picked up a weight before, and empathy is the same way. Small, consistent efforts matter more than rare, dramatic gestures. This can help you feel confident that you can improve your empathy step by step.

Building empathy is more like training for a 5K than running a marathon overnight. Instead of making big, dramatic efforts, try small exercises that fit into your daily life. For example, before your next Zoom call or coffee meeting, pause for three minutes. Clear your mind and ask yourself, 'What might this person be dealing with today? If I were in their place, what would feel difficult?' The goal isn't to solve their problems or read their mind. It's about being curious and present, not just going through the motions. You might be surprised how this simple habit helps you focus less on your own concerns and more on connecting with others.

Another helpful exercise is to practice seeing things from someone else's perspective, especially when reading news that upsets you or feels unfamiliar. When you come across an article that frustrates you, pause and try to imagine how someone with a different view might feel. What are they worried about? What experiences might influence their reaction? Even if you don't agree, this mental exercise helps strengthen your empathy. It won't make every disagreement easy, but it will help you handle complex situations and connect with others.

You don't need a lot of extra time to practice empathy. Small, everyday interactions are great opportunities. If you notice a coworker sighing or looking down during a meeting, gently mention what you see: 'You look a little stressed today. Is anything on your mind?' This isn't nosy; it shows you care. At the coffee shop, instead of just placing your order, take a moment to ask the barista how their day is going. When they answer, really listen instead of just nodding and moving on. These small moments are like mini-workouts for your empathy, helping you feel more connected and confident in your ability to support others.

Research supports this idea. Studies show that small acts, such as taking another person's perspective and checking in on others, can improve emotional intelligence, job satisfaction, and teamwork. When people feel noticed, even briefly, they are more likely to trust you and share more in the future. Over time, these small actions can change the environment around you. Plus, it feels good to know you've made someone's day a little better.

Rate Your Empathy Muscle

Take two minutes for this quick check-in:

- On a scale from 1 (rarely) to 5 (often), how often do you pause to consider someone else's feelings before reacting?

- In the past week, did you check in on someone's mood or ask a thoughtful follow-up question?

- When did you last assume positive intent, choosing to believe someone meant well even if they annoyed you?

- How often do you seek out perspectives from people outside your usual circle?

Write down your answers or think about them. There's no need to judge yourself; this is just a way to notice where you might want to strengthen your empathy.

Thinking about these small actions helps you see your progress over time. Maybe last month you rarely paused before reacting in meetings, but now you do it once or twice a week. That's something to celebrate. If you notice yourself falling back into old habits or judging quickly, see it as feedback, not failure.

The key is to be consistent. Try to include one act of empathy in your day, like taking a three-minute pause before a meeting, checking in with a friend or stranger, or trying to see another side of something that bothers you. Over time, your empathy will grow, and the world around you will feel more connected and human. This can help you feel hopeful that small, regular actions lead to meaningful change.

Validating Emotions, How to Show You "Get It" (Even If You Disagree)

You might think that validating someone's emotions means giving in or just agreeing with them, but that's not the case. Validation and agreement are not the same. To validate is to recognize and accept someone's feelings, even if you would choose differently or have another opinion. Everyone wants to feel understood, especially when they're upset. Still, during arguments or tense moments, it's easy to skip over feelings and jump straight to logic, solutions, or defending yourself.

Imagine a situation where a teenager slams their door and shouts about an unfair curfew. The parent might feel attacked and want to argue or end the conversation. But there's another way. The parent could pause and say, 'It sounds like you're really angry about this rule. I get that it feels unfair.' They aren't agreeing to change the curfew or saying the yelling is okay; they're just naming the emotion. This can help the teen calm down and keep talking. Validating emotions doesn't mean you think someone is right about everything; it means you understand why they feel that way.

In tense moments, it helps to use words that build understanding. When emotions are high, try saying, 'I can see why that would be upsetting,' or 'It makes sense you'd feel that way.' These simple phrases don't fix the problem or excuse mistakes, but they open the door to real conversation. During a tough feedback session at work, pay attention to emotional signals, like a colleague's tense voice or hunched shoulders. Instead of pushing forward, pause and say, 'I see this feedback is landing hard. I appreciate you sticking with me.' This isn't sugarcoating; it's being honest about what's happening.

Sometimes, what people say is only part of what they feel. Imagine a friend sitting quietly after hearing bad news, looking down and not moving much. You might sense sadness or anger but not know what to do. Instead of filling the silence or changing the subject, try saying, 'I can tell this hit you hard. I'm here if you want to talk about it, or if you'd rather not.' This shows you notice both what's said and what isn't.

Sometimes, trying to validate someone's feelings doesn't go as planned. A sibling might say, 'You don't really understand,' or a coworker might say, 'That's not what I meant.' Your first reaction might be to defend yourself, but try not to. Instead, say, 'You're right, I might not fully get it yet, but I want to understand better. Can you help me see what I'm missing?' This keeps the conversation on track without making things worse. People may want to see if you're sincere before they trust you, so patience is important.

Defensiveness can make these moments harder. Sometimes, when you try to validate, the other person responds with sarcasm or pulls away. If that happens, take a step back and focus on making things feel safe again, rather than trying to solve everything right away. You can say, 'If I'm off-base, let me know. I'm here to listen.' Or offer a break: 'We can pause if this is too much right now.' Validation isn't a quick fix; it's a gentle way to encourage openness.

Validation also means paying close attention to body language. Notice things like clenched jaws, crossed arms, or someone avoiding eye contact; these can be signs that emotions are building up, even if they seem calm. Respond with curiosity, not blame: 'You seem quieter than usual. Anything on your mind?' This simple recognition can help prevent defensiveness from getting worse.

When conversations stall, or emotions run high, go back to the basics: listen first, repeat what you hear and notice, and check in gently without assuming you got it right the first time. Over time, these small actions build trust and make it safer for people to share tough feelings. People don't need you to fix everything; they want to feel seen and accepted for how they really feel.

Validation works in nearly every relationship, whether it's a family argument, a disagreement at work, or a friendship going through a rough patch. You don't have to agree with everything or give up your own boundaries. You need to show that someone's feelings matter enough for you to notice and name them honestly. Often, that's enough to turn defensiveness into real conversation and keep your connection strong.

Holding Space, Creating Safety for Vulnerable Conversations

Holding space isn't just sitting back and doing nothing. It's an active, intentional effort. You're not trying to fix things, take control, or give advice unless someone asks for it. Instead, you choose to be fully present so the other person can share what they're really going through. Many people think holding space means being hands-off, but it's actually about creating a safe, judgment-free place where someone can let their guard down. There's a big difference between trying to fix someone's pain and simply witnessing it. Fixing can make someone feel small or misunderstood, while witnessing lets their experience stand on its own.

To create a safe space, start by removing distractions that undermine trust. Put your phone on silent and out of sight. Turn off the TV, step away from your laptop, and do whatever you need so your attention is fully on the other person. Even a buzzing watch can interrupt a meaningful conversation. The setting matters more than we think; a quiet room or a walk outside can help. Once you're present, pay attention to your body language. Keep your posture open, relax your shoulders, and uncross your arms. Lean in a little to show you're engaged. Make eye contact that feels warm, rest your hands calmly, and nod gently to show you're listening.

Handling discomfort is important because tough conversations are rarely easy. There might be long silences, tears, or even anger. It's normal to want to jump in and fix things or offer advice right away, but try to hold back. Let the other person cry, vent, or sit quietly if that's what they need. Sometimes, just being there is enough, even if you're both silent after someone shares something difficult. These pauses give emotions time to settle and show you're not afraid of strong feelings. With practice, you'll see that quiet support can mean more than any comforting words.

Setting the tone at the start of a vulnerable conversation is helpful. Using simple scripts isn't about sounding stiff; it gives you a gentle guide when emotions are strong or words are hard to find. You can start with, 'Is now a good time to talk? I want to be fully present for you.' This shows your intent and lets the other person say no if they're not ready. You could also say, 'I care about you and want to listen without distractions. Should we sit somewhere quiet?' These small steps help build trust from the beginning.

When emotions spill over or tough truths come out, don't rush to close down the conversation or make it tidy. Sit with whatever comes up, even if it's uncomfortable for you as the listener. If the other person falls silent after sharing something painful, avoid filling the void with platitudes or nervous chatter. Instead, try a soft acknowledgment: "Thank you for trusting me with this. I'm here if you want to share more, or if you want some company." Sometimes people need permission to sit with their feelings before moving forward.

Ending these conversations with care is just as important as how you start them. When it feels like things are winding down, gently check in: "Do you want to talk more now, or take a break?" Or reassure them: "I'm here if anything else comes up, no pressure." If it's been especially heavy, offer a simple thank-you: "It means a lot that you shared this with me." These bookends give structure to something that might otherwise feel overwhelming or unfinished.

Holding space is an active choice, a commitment to witness rather than rescue, to trust that another person's story deserves room to breathe even if it's messy or unresolved. When you show up this way, you become someone others turn to in moments of real need, not because you have all the answers, but because you know how to make space for their truth to unfold.

Boundaries for the Caring Listener, Helping Without Absorbing

Caring deeply for others can be both rewarding and overwhelming. Supporting a friend through a rough time can easily turn into lying awake replaying their worries as if they're your own. The line between empathy (feeling with someone) and emotional entanglement (absorbing their pain) is thin and easy to cross. Boundaries are essential; they're not barriers, but fences that protect your own well-being while you care for others. Without them, empathy can become draining, leaving you exhausted, frazzled, and even resentful. If you've ever left a conversation feeling mentally heavy or noticed carrying someone else's stress long after they're gone, you've likely crossed from empathy into enmeshment.

Early warning signs of emotional overload are often subtle. Physical tension, obsessing over how to "fix" someone's problems, snapping at unrelated people, or crashing in energy after supporting others can all be clues. Sometimes, you may feel inexplicably drained for days, or dread calls from someone struggling, or even feel guilty for wanting alone time. These aren't failures of compassion; they signal your boundaries need attention.

You don't have to wait until you're depleted to set boundaries. Before engaging in an emotionally charged talk, pause and ask yourself: "How am I feeling right now? Do I have the capacity to listen?" It's okay to be honest about your limits. Saying, "I want to support you, but if I get overwhelmed, I may need to pause," sets clear expectations and allows for much-needed breaks. According to a TIME report, clearly stating your needs helps protect your mental well-being and maintain a compassionate environment.

Setting Practical Boundaries

A TIME report suggests that setting time limits during challenging conversations can be a supportive way to establish practical boundaries. It's not unkind to say, "I have 20 minutes to focus on you." This keeps expectations clear and takes away any guilt if you need to step away. If more needs to be said once time is up, suggest picking it up later: "I wish I could give more right now, can we check in again tomorrow when I'm fresh?" These small boundaries protect your energy and ensure you can show up fully.

Reset with Self-Care

After difficult talks, self-care isn't optional; it's necessary to maintain your emotional health. Get outside, breathe deeply, journal for five minutes, or move your body to signal to yourself that the conversation is over. Splash cold water on your face or literally shake out your limbs if it helps. Remind yourself: caring doesn't mean carrying everything.

Saying No with Kindness

It's difficult to tell someone you can't take on their emotions, especially if they're hurting. But saying no is kinder than pretending you can listen when you're spent. Use simple scripts: "I care about you, but I'm not in the right headspace tonight. Can we talk tomorrow when I can give you my full attention?" Or, "I want to give this what it deserves, but I need a little space first." These phrases put honesty first without shaming anyone.

Boundaries Make Empathy Sustainable

Boundaries are not just about limiting access; they help you show up at your best. Setting them takes practice, and may feel awkward if you're used to being everyone's go-to listener. But protecting your energy allows empathy to become something that fills both sides, yours and theirs, instead of just draining you.

Sometimes people push back against your limits, expressing disappointment or guilt ("But you always listen," or "I really need you right now"). Hold steady: "I care deeply, and that's why I need to pause before I can be helpful." Consistent, kind boundaries teach others to respect your limits, and often, people appreciate the clarity.

Learning your own limits reshapes how you relate to others' pain. You stay compassionate without losing yourself in someone else's story. That's not selfishness, it's self-respect, and it keeps empathy alive for the long term.

Empathy in Action, Scripts for Grief, Crisis, and Tough Times

When someone you care about is grieving or in crisis, finding the right words can feel impossible. You want to help, but it's easy to freeze or worry about saying the wrong thing. In these moments, simple and honest scripts are best. Saying, "I'm so sorry you're going through this. I'm here to listen," signals your presence and willingness to stay with their feelings, even if you can't fix the pain. Sometimes, offering a choice can help: "Would you like to talk about what happened, or would you prefer some company in silence?" This lets them control the conversation and go at their own pace.

It's common to reach for comforting clichés like "Everything happens for a reason" or "At least they're in a better place." While well-intentioned, these comments can feel dismissive of their pain or suggest moving on too quickly. Similarly, making it about your own experiences, "I know exactly how you feel", often shifts the focus away from them. Instead, pause before responding and center your words on their experience. If you're unsure what to say, it's okay to admit it: "I wish I had the perfect words, but I care about you."

Support isn't always about advice or action. Often, your quiet presence matters most. After a breakup or loss, you don't need to fill every moment with pep talks or distractions. Just sitting together in silence, passing tissues, or letting a friend cry can be incredibly comforting. If you're far away, a simple text like "Thinking of you. No need to reply" shows you care without putting pressure on them to respond.

A common oversight is disappearing after the initial crisis. People often receive support right away, but as days pass and attention fades, the hurt lingers. According to research by Depow, Francis, and Inzlicht, adults experience multiple opportunities to show empathy during daily life, so setting a reminder to check in with someone by saying, "Hey, I've been thinking about you," can help you take advantage of these moments of connection. Want to grab coffee or hang out?" Gently mentioning their loss honors their ongoing pain. Sharing a brief memory about their loved one, like "I was just remembering when your dad told that joke at your birthday, it always makes me smile," acknowledges that their person mattered and isn't forgotten.

Empathy means respecting boundaries, too. If someone doesn't seem ready to talk, say, "I get that you may not want to talk now, just know I'm here if or when you do." Support isn't about the quantity of advice you give, but about how safe and seen you make people feel.

Asking What Helps

It helps to ask directly what would be supportive: "Is there something specific I can do, or would it help more just to have me around?" Don't assume everyone wants the same kind of comfort; some people want to talk, others want distraction or space. Clear, gentle questions work better than tiptoeing around the obvious.

The Power of Steady Presence

Over time, your reliability is what really helps, not fancy words or big gestures. If weeks go by and your friend is still hurting, a message like, "No pressure to reply, just wanted to remind you I'm still here," can be just what they need to feel less alone.

In summary, the real gift is your willingness to stay with someone through their tough times, without rushing or trying to fix everything. Empathy isn't about taking on everyone's pain; it's about showing up with patience, honesty, and openness, even when things are difficult or awkward. These scripts and mindsets lay the groundwork for trust and a deeper connection. As you tackle listening barriers, keep them in mind; they will help foster stronger relationships wherever you go.

Chapter Five

Navigating Listening Barriers

Multitasking Mayhem: How to Stay Present Amid Digital Distractions

Have you ever tried having a real conversation while your phone keeps buzzing and notifications pop up nonstop? That's the reality of multitasking today. Maybe you're on a Zoom call, looking at slides, when your email pings and Slack dings, and suddenly someone asks you a question. You scramble to catch up, hoping your face doesn't show that your mind was somewhere else. This happens to everyone. We like to think we can handle it all, but multitasking with technology actually hurts our focus, memory, and relationships.

Here's why this matters. Research shows that switching between digital tasks can cut your productivity by up to 40%. Even just having your phone on the table, without using it, can lower your cognitive skills by as much as 20%. When you jump between apps or check texts while someone is talking, your attention is divided. You miss small cues, like a friend's tone or a coworker's worried look. Over time, this can damage trust. People notice when you're not fully present, and your memory suffers too: in one study, half of the adults couldn't remember a ten-minute talk right after hearing it.

It's more than just missing details. When you only half-listen, people can feel ignored. You might miss a friend's frustration or a partner's quiet request for support because you were distracted by a notification. That feeling can last; it's the difference between feeling valued and feeling invisible. Digital distractions are everywhere. Workspaces are full of "notification hotspots," with phones lighting up, laptops chiming, and TVs flickering. Even at home, the dining table might be a charging station or a place to check the news.

How can you regain control? Start by checking your digital habits and your environment before important conversations. Do a quick "tech hygiene" check: Is your phone nearby? Are there open browser tabs that might distract you? Are smart speakers making noise in the background? Notice where distractions tend to gather, like the kitchen counter, car dashboard, or your desk, and how they pull your attention away from the person in front of you. Sometimes, even a smartwatch buzzing every few minutes can be the biggest distraction.

Before important conversations, whether it's a work meeting or a family talk, take a moment to prepare. Silence your phone or turn on "Do Not Disturb." Put your devices face down or, if you can, put them in another room. Close any apps or browser windows you don't need. If you're working from home, arrange your screen so you only see what you need for the conversation. These small changes show both you and the other person that they have your full attention.

Focusing on one thing at a time is the best way to fight the chaos of multitasking. Create simple habits to help you stay present. At the start of a meeting, let others know you're muting notifications to focus. With family, try using a "tech basket" where everyone puts their phones away before dinner or during important conversations. Some people also schedule "no-device" time on their calendars, setting aside thirty minutes for real, uninterrupted connection.

Distractions will still happen sometimes. You don't have to feel bad when they do. Instead, try quick habits to get back on track. One helpful tip is to name the distraction out loud: "Sorry, my mind wandered for a second, let me come back." This helps both you and the other person reset and keeps things honest without making anyone uncomfortable. Another simple trick is the "one deep breath" rule: when you notice your focus slipping, pause for a slow breath in and out before returning to the conversation. This small break helps your brain refocus.

Your Digital Distraction Audit

Take two minutes before your next important conversation. Write down every device or app within arm's reach and note which ones tend to interrupt you most (phone calls, Slack, news alerts). Then try removing or silencing just one of these before you begin talking. Afterward, jot down how much more present you felt and whether the other person noticed an improvement.

Remember, no one gets this right all the time. The goal isn't to cut yourself off from technology, but to make small changes that add up. Every moment you're present builds trust and understanding, leading to fewer misunderstandings and stronger connections. People want your attention, not just your words, even when distractions are everywhere.

Taming Your Inner Assumptions, Getting Past Snap Judgments

Most of us think we're good at understanding situations or what others mean, but our brains often fill in the blanks with our own stories. Sometimes, before someone finishes speaking, you've already decided what they mean or what will happen next. This "story in your head" can feel reassuring, but it's often wrong. For example, you might hear a teenager sigh and immediately think it's "drama," getting annoyed without really listening. Or you might assume a quiet coworker is checked out, when they could just be nervous or deep in thought. These quick judgments are subtle and shape how you listen and respond, often without you noticing.

Assumptions aren't just about other people; they're about motives, outcomes, even entire conversations. You expect your boss's feedback to be negative, so every word feels like criticism. Or you assume your partner's complaint is about you, not the hard day they had. The problem? Acting on these snap judgments short-circuits real listening. You start responding to your internal story, not the actual words or feelings being shared. This locks you into misunderstandings and keeps old arguments alive.

You can break this automatic pattern with a simple tool: the "Pause and Check" strategy. When you notice yourself jumping to conclusions, pause and ask, "What am I assuming right now?" Naming your assumption creates space for curiosity. For example, if you think, "She's just overreacting," pause and ask yourself, "Is that true? Or am I missing something?" You can also try to approach each conversation with a "beginner's mind," acting as if you know nothing about what the other person will say. This takes effort, especially in the moment, but it helps you listen better.

Using the right language can help you avoid assumptions in the moment. Instead of pushing your own view, ask for clarification. You might say, "It sounds like you might be upset about the schedule. Is that right, or am I missing something?" Or, "I want to make sure I'm not jumping to conclusions; can you tell me more?" These simple phrases show you're open and willing to listen. They give the other person a chance to correct you or explain, which can change the whole conversation.

It's not enough to catch yourself just once or twice. Pay attention to your personal triggers, the situations or people that make you judge quickly. Maybe you assume things most with family members who push your buttons or with coworkers who communicate differently. Start noticing these moments. After a tough conversation, spend five minutes reflecting: "What was I assuming? Did I let an old story affect how I listened? How might things have gone if I had checked my assumption?" Writing this down can help you spot patterns you might not see otherwise.

Try this journaling prompt after a tough interaction: "Describe a recent time when you realized you'd misjudged someone's intent or meaning. What did you assume? What was actually going on? How did it affect the conversation?" Over time, these entries will reveal blind spots, places where your brain loves to jump ahead without evidence.

Case in point: consider a manager who reads a team member's silence as laziness or disengagement. If that manager pauses and asks for input, "I've noticed you've been quiet in meetings; is there something on your mind?", they might discover the person is overwhelmed or anxious about speaking up, not checked out at all. That pivot changes everything: instead of resentment building on both sides, there's a chance for support, understanding, and maybe even growth.

Noticing your snap judgments isn't about being perfect; it's about making progress. Each time you pause an assumption and ask for clarity, you make real listening possible. Even a small pause can help trust and connection grow. The more you practice, the easier it becomes to notice old habits and replace them with curiosity and real interest. Over time, checking your assumptions will feel natural and help your relationships avoid unnecessary problems.

The Bias Blind Spot, Interrupting Your Own Filter Bubble

If you've ever found yourself agreeing more with certain people or remembering some comments better than others in a meeting, you've experienced the "bias blind spot." This isn't just about obvious stereotypes; it's the tendency to think you're less biased than others, even though everyone filters information through their own preferences. You might believe you're fair, but your brain often favors familiar voices and ideas. Confirmation bias, or the habit of agreeing with those who think like you, can show up in group discussions, making you pay more attention to similar views and ignore different ones.

These mental filters are subtle and quietly affect who gets heard. On a project, I once noticed I paid more attention to a colleague who agreed with me and ignored another's objections, thinking she was just being "difficult." Later, I realized her input could have saved us time and effort. Unconscious bias can happen at home too, where you might favor opinions that match your own or let one family member dominate while quieter voices fade into the background.

To break out of this echo chamber, start by noticing your own filter bubble. After meetings or family talks, do a "voice audit": write down who spoke, who was interrupted, and whose ideas shaped the outcome. Look for patterns, do some voices always dominate or fade away? This can be eye-opening and sometimes humbling, but the goal is to become aware, not to feel guilty.

Once you spot patterns, take practical steps to broaden your perspective. In group settings, assign someone to play "devil's advocate" to challenge group thinking and make disagreement normal and safe, encouraging quieter voices. Rotate who leads discussions so everyone gets a chance, and old power dynamics are broken. Anonymous suggestion boxes can also help people share ideas if they're hesitant to speak up, reducing fear of judgment.

Simple invitations can help as well. If someone hasn't spoken, gently ask, "Do you have thoughts you'd like to share?" or "We haven't heard from you yet. Anything to add?" The goal isn't to force anyone, but to make space for different views. You can also go around the room before moving on to make sure everyone has a chance to speak.

Having a curious mindset when someone disagrees with you is powerful. Instead of quickly dismissing different opinions, pause and ask yourself, "What are they seeing that I'm missing?" Moving from defensiveness to curiosity can help you understand more.

Research shows these efforts work. Teams with different backgrounds, experiences, and voices do better than groups where everyone is similar. They are more creative, solve problems faster, and make better decisions. One study found that companies that encourage diverse opinions and diversity saw real improvements in innovation and financial results. The key is listening; when people feel heard, they take more risks and challenge each other in helpful ways.

I've seen this happen on projects where new perspectives helped avoid big mistakes. For example, a newcomer once pointed out problems no one else noticed, which led to important changes. If we had only listened to familiar voices, we would have missed those valuable insights.

To build these habits, keep track of who speaks most and least in meetings, review this regularly, rotate who leads discussions, or make sure there's at least one different opinion before making decisions. These routines help make varied input normal and reduce bias.

Bias never completely goes away, but you can limit its effects by listening on purpose. Notice who isn't part of the conversation and invite them to join. This leads to better results and helps create a culture where everyone's voice is valued.

Handling Repetition, Listening Well When Others Circle Back

It can be frustrating when conversations keep circling back to the same topic, whether it's a coworker stuck on a small policy, a friend bringing up an old issue, or a family member worrying about the same thing again and again. We often call this rambling, but repetition usually means something deeper. People repeat themselves because they feel anxious or unheard, or because they want to stress what matters most to them. When they bring up a topic again, they often want acknowledgment, reassurance, or validation, not just advice or information.

It's easy to get impatient or stop listening when conversations repeat. Your mind wants to fix the problem, move on, or check out. Instead, try to notice what's behind the repetition. Is there an unspoken worry, growing tension, or a need for comfort? Listen for the feelings underneath. For example, a coworker who keeps bringing up a work issue might be afraid of losing control or being ignored. A partner who talks about a past disagreement may want to know you understand their pain. Often, repetition is about wanting to be seen and taken seriously, not just the topic itself.

To break this cycle without making someone feel dismissed, focus on the emotional need behind the topic. Ask gentle questions like, "What feels most important about this right now?" or "I notice we've talked about this a few times, what's still on your mind?" These questions show you care about their feelings, not just the topic, and encourage more meaningful conversations.

Simple phrases can help too. You could say, "I hear that this is really important to you. Is there something specific you'd like me to do or know?" This shows you're listening and lets them explain what they need, whether it's advice or just someone to listen. If the conversation feels stuck, try, "We've talked about this a few times. Would it help to brainstorm solutions together?" This way, you show you care and gently move the conversation toward action or resolution.

Sometimes people don't realize they're repeating themselves. A gentle prompt like, "You've mentioned this a couple of times, and I want to make sure I'm understanding. What's at the heart of it for you?" shows you're paying attention and helps them explain what's really going on.

In groups or at work, repetition can take up time and slow things down. Use tools that keep things respectful and efficient. For example, summarize and write down key points: "Let's jot down your main concerns so we can address them together." This shows you're listening but avoids endless discussion. Another helpful tactic is a "parking lot", a shared notepad or digital document for discussing ongoing issues later. You can say, "That's an important point, let's add it to our list to revisit after today's agenda." This way, the speaker feels heard, and the meeting stays on track.

Clear but kind boundaries are important when time is short. For example, you might say, "I see this matters, but we have ten minutes left. Can we agree on one next step before we finish?" In personal situations, if a friend is stuck on an old story, respond warmly and honestly: "I know this still bothers you. Want to talk about how we can move forward together?" This helps you both find a solution without ignoring their feelings.

Repetition usually isn't random; it often shows deeper needs or feelings that want to be recognized. Paying attention to what's underneath and using words that show both empathy and direction can help everyone feel understood and keep the conversation moving. Most of the time, people don't want you to fix their problem; they want to know that what matters to them matters to you. This small change can turn repeated conversations into meaningful ones where everyone feels respected and heard.

Managing Emotional Hijacks, Staying Grounded in High-Stress Talks

When emotions run high, even good listeners can lose focus. You might feel your heart race or your jaw tighten, and suddenly it's hard to listen. You might snap in an argument or shut down before hearing the whole story. This isn't just bad luck or your personality; it's how your brain works. Neuroscience calls this an "amygdala hijack." The amygdala, a small part deep in your brain, acts like a smoke alarm. When it senses a threat, real or not, it floods your body with stress hormones and triggers a fight-or-flight response. Instead of calmly listening, you're ready to defend, attack, or escape. Clear thinking fades, and survival mode takes over.

Think about the last time a conversation got tense, and you reacted before you realized it. Maybe you snapped at a partner over something small, or your mind went blank in a tough meeting. That rush of heat and urge to interrupt or pull away is a classic amygdala hijack. In these moments, your instincts push you to act, but what you really need is to stay present and patient. Listening is almost impossible unless you find ways to ground yourself.

Grounding techniques aren't just for yogis or therapists; they're practical tools anyone can use in the middle of a tough talk. One of the most effective is "box breathing." It's simple: inhale slowly for four counts, hold for four, exhale for four, hold again for four, and repeat. This method does more than calm you down; it signals to your nervous system that you're safe, pulling you out of panic mode. If breathwork isn't your thing, try anchoring yourself physically: grip a pen, press your feet firmly to the floor, or run your fingers along the edge of your chair. These small physical cues can snap you back into the present and help you ride out the storm without saying something you'll regret.

You can also use quick self-talk prompts to catch yourself in real time. Try silently repeating, "This is just a conversation," or "I can pause before I react." Sometimes naming what's happening to yourself, "I notice my chest feels tight", is enough to slow things down and put you back in control. If things are escalating, don't be afraid to say it out loud: "I notice I'm feeling really tense right now, can we pause for a moment?" or "It seems like this is a really charged topic, how can we talk about it safely?" These statements do two things at once: they acknowledge the emotion in the room and invite everyone to take a breath together. You'll be surprised how quickly tension drops when someone calls out what everyone is already feeling.

A big part of managing emotional hijacks is learning to recognize them early and take action before things spiral. But even if you slip up, if you raise your voice or say something sharp, you can still repair the conversation after the fact. In fact, reflecting on what triggered you is where real learning happens. After a heated exchange, grab a notebook and answer honestly: "What set me off? What was I feeling right before I lost my cool? What could I try differently next time?" This isn't about beating yourself up; it's about collecting data so that next time, you spot the warning signs sooner.

If you need to repair things with someone else, keep it simple. A follow-up apology or reset statement goes a long way: "I'm sorry I got defensive earlier, I care about what you're saying and want to try again." Or even just, "Can we have a do-over? I wasn't listening as well as I wanted to." Most people aren't looking for perfection; they're looking for honesty and effort.

Emotional hijacks happen to everyone. The trick isn't avoiding them entirely; it's catching them early and learning how to recover when they do sneak up on you. Over time, these moments become less frequent and less intense as you build new habits for staying grounded.

Emotional Check-In

After your next tough conversation, no matter how it goes, grab a pen and write for five minutes: What emotions did I notice in myself? What helped me stay grounded (or lose my grip)? What would I like to try next time? These notes will help you spot patterns and build new responses over time.

Wrapping up this chapter, remember that listening barriers are normal but not permanent. Every time you catch yourself and reset, even mid-conversation, you're building trust with others and your confidence. Up next, we'll explore how nonverbal cues can help you listen better, even when words fall short.

Chapter Six

Nonverbal Listening, Reading, and Sending the Right Signals

Eye Contact, Nods, and Posture: The Body Language of Real Attention

Your body sends messages before you say a word. Picture meeting a friend at a busy café. You lean in, make eye contact, and nod as they talk about a problem. Your actions show you're really listening, making the other person feel valued and understood. Now imagine you're looking at your phone, arms crossed, and glancing at the door. Even if you say you're listening, your body says otherwise. This silent exchange builds trust, comfort, and openness. It's not magic; it's the science of nonverbal cues.

Eye contact is an important signal. Meeting someone's gaze, without staring, shows respect and interest. In Western cultures, it often means confidence and honesty, and people tend to trust you more if you look them in the eye. However, not all cultures see eye contact the same way. In many East Asian cultures, direct eye contact with elders or authority figures can be perceived as disrespectful or aggressive. Looking down or away can show politeness or humility. Try not to judge someone for avoiding eye contact. Instead, match their comfort level, soften your gaze, or look away when they do.

Nodding is a simple way to keep a conversation moving. A gentle nod says, "I understand, go on." It reassures and encourages, especially when words aren't needed. Nodding should feel natural, though. If you nod too much, it can come across as impatient or even mocking. In emotional conversations, well-timed nods help others feel safe to share.

Posture is more important than you might realize. Sitting with relaxed shoulders, uncrossed arms, and feet on the floor shows you are open and approachable. Leaning forward during a tough conversation shows you are engaged and paying attention. On the other hand, crossing your arms or leaning away can make you seem defensive or bored, even if that's not your intention. In meetings or one-on-one conversations, ask yourself whether your posture is open and welcoming, or if you might be closed off without noticing.

These signals don't just help others; they help you focus, too. Sitting up straight and leaning in gets your brain ready to pay attention. Keeping steady eye contact and nodding slowly also helps you stay present.

Mirroring helps you connect even more. When you match someone's relaxed posture or how close they sit, it shows you are safe to be around. The key is to be genuine, not to copy every move. Pay attention to their pace, lean back if they do, or lean in if they share something personal. Mirroring helps people feel understood and in sync with you.

Here's an example: picture two parents at a family meeting. One sits upright with open arms, makes gentle eye contact, and nods now and then, showing, "I'm here for you." The other sits back with crossed arms, looking at the TV, showing they are not really engaged. The first parent's body language invites conversation, while the second's can stop it.

Body Language Audit

During your next important conversation, do a quick self-scan:

- Are your arms open or crossed?

- Are your feet planted or fidgeting?

- Is your eye contact soft and steady?

- Do nods feel natural and supportive?

- Are you leaning in or pulling away? Changing just one of these signals can make a big difference in how comfortable and open the other person feels.

Remember, real attention usually shows in your body before you say anything. Every time you lean forward, make an open gesture, or give a real nod, you're telling someone "You matter" before you offer any advice or answers.

Voice Tone and Pace, What You Hear Beyond Words

When you call a friend, you can often tell how they feel just by hearing their voice for a few seconds, even before they finish saying hello. The tone, volume, and speed of someone's speech carry a lot of emotional information, sometimes more than the words themselves. These cues are always present in conversations. Some people notice them easily, but anyone can get better at picking them up with practice.

Tone shows the emotion behind your words. It's not just about being loud or quiet, but about the feeling you share. A warm, steady tone helps build trust and comfort, making the listener feel more confident. A sharp or cold tone, even if your words are polite, can push people away. For example, if you slow down and speak more quietly during a disagreement, it can help calm things down. Raising your voice can show urgency or anger, while speaking softly can calm others or, if used too much in tense moments, might seem like you're avoiding the issue.

How fast you speak also affects how your message comes across. Talking too quickly can make you seem nervous or impatient, especially when things are tense. Slowing down gives others time to think, shows patience, and lets them know you're not trying to take over. If you match someone else's pace, pause when they pause, or slow down if they do, it can make the conversation feel more comfortable and natural. This isn't copying, but finding a rhythm together to build a connection, making everyone feel more at ease.

Explain that listening for emotions like sarcasm or fear in voice tone helps you better understand underlying feelings, making your responses more empathetic and accurate.

The real message often comes through in tone and speed, not just words. If someone says "I'm not upset" but their voice cracks or they speak quickly, you can tell there's more going on. Paying attention to these cues helps you avoid misunderstandings and notice what really matters.

Changing your own voice on purpose can quickly change a conversation. If someone is upset and talking fast, try lowering your voice and slowing down to help them calm down. In tense moments, pausing before you answer can help everyone relax, since people often match your energy and speed. To show empathy, use a gentle tone, speak slowly, and don't rush to reply.

Here's an exercise: next time you listen to a voicemail or a recorded meeting, don't focus on the words right away. Close your eyes and ask yourself, "What mood do I hear?", maybe stressed, excited, or annoyed. Write down three words about the tone before you listen to the message itself. This helps you get better at noticing feelings that words might not show.

Another helpful tip is to practice pausing on purpose instead of filling silences with "uh" or "um." When you feel like using a filler, just pause and take a breath. Silence gives both you and the other person time to think, which can lead to more honest and meaningful conversations.

You'll soon see how these changes affect people. Friends may share more when you respond to their real feelings. Coworkers will feel calmer if you keep your voice steady during stressful times. Family arguments often cool down when people pause before answering. With practice, noticing tone and pace becomes natural, like reading between the lines with your ears.

How we sound, our tone, speed, and volume, shape trust and understanding before and after we speak. Noticing these vocal cues and adjusting your own is more than just good listening. It's a powerful way to build a real connection in any conversation.

When Words and Signals Clash, Repairing Mixed Messages

We've all seen times when someone says, "I'm fine," but their tight jaw or averted eyes tell a different story. Or maybe a coworker smiles while giving bad news, but their hands grip the podium. These are mixed messages when words and body language don't match. Even if people can't say exactly what's wrong, they often feel something is off, which can make conversations uncomfortable.

Mixed messages can happen anywhere. At home, your partner might say everything is fine, but their voice sounds flat, and their shoulders are slumped. Or you might tell your boss you're okay missing a new project, but your arms are crossed. These moments can confuse people and lead to mistrust, since most people place more weight on body language and tone than on words. When our signals don't match, others may think we're hiding something or are not aware of our own feelings.

Spotting and Addressing Mixed Messages

It takes practice and curiosity to notice when words and body language don't match. If you sense a mismatch, like positive words but a tense posture, don't call someone out or make them feel defensive. Instead, gently point out the difference: "You say you're okay, but you look a bit tense. Is there more on your mind?" or "Your words sound upbeat, but I'm sensing something else. Do you want to talk?" The goal isn't to act like a therapist, but to make space for honesty and show that all types of communication matter.

People sometimes worry that mentioning these differences will embarrass others or make things worse. But if you do it kindly and without pressure, most people appreciate the chance to explain or open up. You can say, "I notice your words say one thing, but your energy feels different. Is there anything you want to talk about?" Or reflect, "You're smiling, but this seems like tough news. How are you really?" These small, curious questions help ease tension and encourage honesty.

Turning the Lens Inward

It's important to use this awareness on yourself, too. Everyone sends mixed messages sometimes, often without realizing it. Maybe you tried to sound upbeat in a meeting, but your body language showed disappointment. Or you told friends you were happy to help, but your sighs said otherwise. People usually react more to your signals than your words, and over time, these mismatches can weaken trust.

Before important conversations, do a quick check: Do my words match how I feel? Is my body language in line with what I mean? If not, pause, take a breath, and adjust your words or actions to express your true feelings better. It's not about being perfect, but about being clear enough that others know where you stand.

If a conversation felt off, whether you noticed your own mixed signals or someone else did, take a moment to reflect. Ask yourself: When did I send mixed signals? How did I feel compared to what I said? How did others react? Being honest with yourself helps you be clearer with others. If you realize later that your signals didn't match, fix it with a simple follow-up, like, "Hey, I said I was fine earlier, but I was actually frustrated. Sorry for not being clear." This can help rebuild trust.

Small Shifts, Big Impact

If you notice yourself falling back into old habits, like smiling when you're stressed or saying you're fine while your body says otherwise, pause before you answer. Ask yourself, What am I really feeling? What do I want to share? Even a small step toward honesty can change the conversation. Over time, people will notice and trust both your words and your presence.

When you learn to notice and gently mention mismatched signals, everyone feels safer and more understood. Fixing mixed messages isn't about catching someone being fake or making them share. It's about making space for honesty, even if it feels awkward at first. When signals don't match, it's a chance for clarity and real connection.

Nonverbal Pitfalls in Virtual Meetings, Making Presence Visible on Zoom

Video calls can make you seem less lively and present. Many of the small signals we use in person, like timing, posture, or leaning in, can get lost or misunderstood on screen. If your camera angle is wrong or your face isn't fully visible, you might look distant even if you're paying attention. For example, if only your forehead shows, it can hurt trust and connection before you say anything.

Lighting and camera placement have a big impact on how people see you. If your laptop is your main light, you might look washed out or in shadow, making it hard for others to read your face. Try to sit where natural or lamp light shines on your face, and keep your camera at eye level, even if you have to use books to raise it. This keeps your face centered and shows you're present. When you want to connect or show empathy, look at the camera lens. It might feel strange, but it helps others feel like you're making eye contact and paying attention.

Gestures still matter on video calls. Showing your hands makes what you say more engaging and convincing. Keep your hands in view and use them to highlight points or show you agree. Showing your palms is a sign of openness and honesty. Even small gestures, like leaning in or raising an eyebrow, can make online meetings feel more lively and help people pay attention.

It's easy to look bored during long Zoom meetings. Without trying, you might seem checked out. Keep your facial expressions active: show surprise at big news, smile after a joke, or nod when someone shares an idea. These small reactions let others know you're listening. Lean in a bit when someone shares something personal. This warmth helps build connection, even online.

Multitasking is a common problem in virtual meetings. It's tempting to check emails or your phone, but people notice when your eyes wander or your replies are slow. To avoid this, turn off self-view and set up a "focus zone." Close extra tabs, silence notifications, and remove distractions nearby. Even covering icons with a sticky note can help you stay focused.

Your background matters more than you might expect. Messy laundry or clutter can distract others and make you look less professional. Clean up behind you or use a simple virtual background so people focus on you.

Technical issues like lag and audio delays can make meetings awkward. If there's lag, pause more often and make your nods or smiles bigger so people know you're following. If things get confusing, ask, "Did that come through okay?" to help clarify.

Setting clear expectations for nonverbal engagement can make meetings more lively. For example, teams can agree to stay off mute unless there's background noise, so reactions are more natural. Leaders who use expressive and responsive body language set a good example for everyone.

Don't forget about small digital signals. Wave hello at the start, give a thumbs-up for good news, or keep an open, interested expression while others talk. These small gestures add warmth and make online meetings feel more personal.

If you're not sure how your nonverbal signals look, record a test call or ask a friend for feedback. Check if your gestures are easy to see or if you seem uninterested without meaning to.

Before your next meeting, check a few things: Is your face well-lit? Is your camera at eye level? Can people see your hands? Are your expressions lively and match your mood? Is your background tidy? These small changes help online meetings feel more personal and make sure you're seen and heard.

Tools for Checking In, How to Ask About Unspoken Feelings

Sometimes words aren't enough. You might sit next to a friend and feel that something is wrong, even if they don't say anything. Nonverbal listening helps in these moments, especially when someone is grieving or not ready to talk. Just being there quietly, without pushing for conversation or giving advice, can mean a lot. Sharing silence and showing you don't expect them to feel better right away can be the greatest comfort you offer.

When you do want to reach out, gentle prompts work best. Skip the pressure of "What's wrong?" Instead, try something like, "You seem quiet today, want to talk about what's on your mind?" or "I noticed you haven't said much. I'm here if you want to share." The way you physically position yourself matters too. Sitting side-by-side or at a comfortable angle, rather than face-to-face, eases intensity and feels less like an interrogation. This side-by-side energy can help people open up, especially those who get anxious with confrontation. Small signals like relaxed shoulders or a soft glance invite others to talk at their own pace.

Not everyone finds it easy to put their feelings into words. You probably know someone who clams up when asked how they're doing. For these situations, simple check-in tools can be a game-changer. An "emotion wheel" is a great visual aid; it's a colorful chart listing a wide range of feelings, not just the basics like sad or happy. Lay it on the table during dinner or keep it handy for check-ins at work. Sometimes, all someone needs is to point to an emotion that fits when they can't find the right words. Feeling cards, a stack of cards with different emotions written or pictured on them, serve a similar purpose and make it easier for both adults and kids to communicate what's going on inside.

For those who find even that too much, try a simple rating scale. At the end of a long workday, ask, "How are you, really? On a scale from one to ten?" It's low-pressure and opens the door for a deeper conversation if they feel like it. Sometimes, just saying "I'm about a four today" signals they need support, even when they can't explain why.

One thing that makes these check-ins work is showing your own vulnerability first. If you want people to open up, model it with your own body language and words. Keep your posture relaxed, hands open on your knees or the table, and maintain soft eye contact, never staring, just being available. When you share your own feelings, even briefly, it creates a sense of safety for others to do the same. For example: "Honestly, I've been feeling a bit off myself lately, just wanted to check in with you too." This isn't about making it about yourself; it's about creating space where honesty is welcome.

You'll notice that when you lead with openness, others often follow. They see your comfort with uncertainty and feel less pressure to have tidy answers. Your willingness to show up as imperfect makes room for them to do the same. Even when words fail, or silence lingers, the invitation stands: I'm here, whenever you're ready.

If you'd like to try out some of these tools in real life, here's a quick reflection exercise:

Your Personal Check-In Toolkit

- Think of someone you care about who seems distant lately.

- Which gentle prompt would feel most natural for you? Write it down.

- Would an emotion wheel or feeling cards help in this situation? Maybe a rating scale?

- Notice your own nonverbal cues the next time you check in. Are your shoulders relaxed? Are your hands visible and open? Is your gaze soft?

- After the conversation, jot down what worked and what didn't. Adjust your approach next time.

Checking in is never about fixing someone else's feelings; it's about showing them they matter enough for you to notice and care. Sometimes that's enough to shift the whole tone of a relationship.

As we wrap up this chapter, remember: nonverbal listening gives you access to a deeper understanding and connection than words alone can reach. When you pair gentle questions with an open presence, you build trust that can weather anything. Up next, we'll look at how these listening habits transform workplaces and teams, bringing empathy and clarity into environments where misunderstandings often cost the most.

Chapter Seven

Listening Across Cultures and Contexts

Cultural Listening Norms, What's Polite (Or Rude) Around the World

It's common to feel unsure about what's polite when you're in a new place or with people from different backgrounds. For example, I once greeted Japanese colleagues with direct eye contact and a handshake, which is normal in the U.S. While this shows confidence and respect in America, in Japan, direct eye contact, especially with someone older or higher-ranked, can feel intense or disrespectful. My good intentions made some people uncomfortable. Small cultural cues like this can shape trust before any real conversation starts, highlighting their significance in intercultural communication.

Cultural listening norms exist everywhere, but we often only notice them when we make a mistake. In Mediterranean places like Italy or Greece, lively conversations with hand gestures, raised voices, and frequent interruptions show excitement and engagement. At a family dinner in Naples, everyone talks at once, and interruptions are not rude; they mean people are involved. In contrast, in Sweden or Finland, silence is valued. In these Nordic cultures, pauses are seen as thoughtful and respectful rather than awkward. Filling every quiet moment can come across as impatient or pushy. What feels like silence to you might be a sign of respect to someone else.

Gestures and body language can mean different things in different cultures. Nodding might show agreement in some places, but in others, it just means, "I'm listening." For example, a U.S. manager once thought a Korean team member's nods and silence meant agreement. For the Korean, being quiet and indirect was a way to show respect for authority, not a lack of ideas. Misreading these cues can cause problems in projects or relationships.

It's easy to think your own cultural habits are the norm, but this can hurt trust and teamwork. For example, Americans might see Russian colleagues' lack of small talk as rude, not realizing it's just a different style. Likewise, someone from a direct culture might think a British coworker is avoiding the issue if they use polite language to soften criticism.

One common mistake in cross-cultural situations is seeing silence as a problem. Americans, who often fill pauses, might think silence means someone isn't interested. But in many cultures, such as Japan, China, or Finland, silence shows reflection and respect. Interrupting these pauses can seem disrespectful and make teamwork harder. Recognizing these specific cultural differences in silence can improve your ability to listen inclusively.

To avoid these mistakes, approach new cultural situations with curiosity and humility, making your audience feel safe and open to learning from differences. Before important meetings or partnerships, take a few minutes to review basic etiquette in online guides or business resources. Learn what gestures or silences mean in the culture you're working with. Even if you're not traveling, multicultural teams bring these differences into every interaction, whether in person or online.

Start by observing: notice who speaks quickly, who waits, and who is quiet but paying attention. If someone seems engaged but silent, invite them to share by asking, "Would you like to add something?" This approach helps your audience feel valued and included. Over time, you'll notice patterns in how people prefer to communicate and can adjust your style to connect better. This isn't about changing who you are; it's about building understanding and respect.

Culture Clash Reflection

Think back to a time when you felt out of sync talking with someone from a different background. Maybe there was an awkward pause, or someone seemed distant or too direct. Reflect on what happened, how you responded, and if you were seeing things only from your own perspective. Consider what the other person might have been experiencing. Next time, pause and notice before reacting, you might find new chances to understand each other, fostering empathy and connection.

When you approach conversations with curiosity rather than assumptions, cultural differences become opportunities to build trust and work together. Paying attention to small cues like pauses, nods, gestures, and silences helps you understand what's really being said, no matter the situation or culture.

Generational Differences, Bridging Gaps with Respectful Curiosity

If you've ever been with family, your dad making plans on the phone, your teenage cousin replying with only emojis, your aunt sending lots of links, you've seen generational communication differences up close. Each age group has its own comfort zone. Baby Boomers and many Gen Xers like phone calls or in-person chats, valuing tone and eye contact. Millennials might use voice notes or memes. Gen Z prefers group texts, abbreviations, and emojis, sometimes having whole conversations with just symbols or "lol." For them, an emoji can say more than a sentence. It's not just about convenience; it's about comfort and being real. A phone call might feel intrusive to a twenty-year-old, while a long email can seem too formal to a teen.

These differences often lead to misunderstandings. A manager might see a younger colleague texting during a meeting and think it's disrespectful, even though the person might be looking up notes or clarifying something in a group chat. For them, multitasking is efficient, not rude. An older coworker's call after hours can feel disruptive to someone who values their personal time. Parents might think short replies are rude, while teens see "k" as just "message received." Using devices can make it look like people aren't paying attention, but it's often just a habit or another way to stay connected.

Language changes as well. Slang and informal speech might confuse some people and amuse others. Words like "bet," "no cap," or "sus" aren't lazy, they show belonging for digital natives. On the other hand, being called "sir" or "ma'am" can feel too formal to those who grew up casually. Even punctuation can send mixed signals; a period at the end of a text might seem abrupt or even passive-aggressive to some young adults.

Bridging these gaps doesn't mean you have to pretend to be someone else. Start with curiosity and openness, and don't assume someone means harm just because they do things differently. Try asking, "I notice we share information differently, can we talk about what works best for us?" In families, you might ask, "Do you prefer a text before I call?" or "How should I check in when you're busy?" Small changes can build respect, like sending your mom an email recap after a call or adding a smiley to your niece's texts.

This approach works in the workplace, too. If your team has different preferences, some like real-time discussions, others prefer written updates, try rotating tools. Use Slack for quick check-ins, video calls for big decisions, and emails or docs for reference. Don't be afraid to say, "I'm new to this app, can someone help?" Being honest shows respect and encourages others to do the same.

Try bridging gaps by code-switching. For a week, use your team's chat app for daily updates, even if it feels strange at first. Notice how people react when you change your style. In family chats, reply in the same tone or format as others, respond to a meme with a meme, or ask what they prefer. When talking in person, put your phone away if older relatives value your attention, and later follow up with a text if younger family members prefer that.

Mirroring isn't about copying others; it shows you care enough to meet people halfway. If you're not sure about someone's preference, ask: "Do you like texts, or do you prefer to talk in person?" Listen without judging. Your twelve-year-old cousin might share more over text than at dinner, and your boss might prefer a calendar invite instead of a casual message.

Here's a simple exercise: Make a list of how your family, friends, and coworkers prefer to communicate. Next time you reach out, use their preferred style and see if you notice any changes in how quickly they respond, their mood, or their level of engagement.

With practice, code-switching and being curious get easier. What once felt awkward will become natural, and you'll build respect and understanding across generations.

Navigating Power Dynamics, Listening Up, Down, and Sideways

Power affects how people listen in almost every situation, whether you're talking to a CEO, teaching a class, or leading a family discussion. When power isn't balanced, there's often tension, sometimes obvious, sometimes not. If you've ever felt nervous speaking up around your boss, you know how quickly the pressure rises. "Listening up" often means watching for cues, choosing words carefully, and sometimes holding back ideas that feel risky. I've seen myself and others nod along in meetings, even with doubts, just because the boss is in the room. People often filter their opinions, soften feedback, or agree to avoid conflict. Over time, this can create a culture in which honest ideas are buried, and real problems go unspoken.

When you're in charge, like managing a team or leading a class, the situation changes. "Listening down" means asking for input from people who might not feel safe speaking up. It's easy to think silence means agreement, but often it means people are being careful or afraid of consequences. Employees and students may hold back their real thoughts, worried about being honest. If you want real feedback, you have to work for it. I've found that saying, "Tell me what I'm missing here," can help, but it's not always enough. Power can make people hold back before they even speak.

Listening to peers has its own challenges. Conversations between coworkers at the same level or siblings can quickly become competitive or territorial. Even without a clear leader, subtle power games decide who gets heard and whose words matter most. Who speaks first? Who gets interrupted? Who ends the conversation? These small details show the hidden power dynamics in every group.

A common problem is deference. In meetings, people wait for the leader's opinion before sharing their own or repeating what's already been said. Honest feedback disappears as people second-guess themselves: "Is this safe to say?" "Will I look foolish?" People filter their thoughts without realizing it. In families, kids might stay quiet around parents, and younger siblings copy older ones to avoid conflict.

If you want to make sure everyone is heard, you need to be proactive. Creating psychological safety, where people feel safe to share honestly, takes more than just encouragement. It starts with small habits that invite input from everyone. In meetings, I like to start with a round-robin: "Let's go around so everyone gets a chance to weigh in." If someone is quiet, I'll say, "I'd like to hear from those who haven't spoken yet." This shows that every voice matters, not just the loudest or most senior.

Leaders who show vulnerability help break down barriers quickly. Admitting, "I struggle with listening when I'm stressed, I'm working on it," encourages others to share their own struggles. When a boss admits to missing something or asks for feedback on their own behavior, it shows that honesty is welcome. In classrooms, teachers use anonymous question boxes so even shy students can be heard. At work, some teams use digital surveys or suggestion forms so people can share without worrying about backlash.

Having a script can help when you're nervous. Try saying, "Let's do a quick check-in. I want to make sure we haven't missed any concerns." Or, "If anyone has an idea we haven't covered yet, now's your chance." Sometimes just asking, "What are we not talking about that we should be?" can open up an honest conversation.

Rituals are important too. Rotate who leads meetings so everyone gets a chance to guide the group, let junior staff go first instead of last. Encourage disagreement, not to argue, but because better ideas come from healthy debate. In families, assign chores through open discussion rather than just giving orders, and let everyone share what they find fair.

Power dynamics won't go away overnight, but showing people you truly want to hear them makes a difference. When people feel listened to, whether they're above, below, or beside you, they get more involved. They share new ideas, point out risks sooner, and trust grows stronger for everyone.

Inclusive Listening, Ensuring Every Voice Is Heard

Inclusive listening means making a real effort to hear and value everyone, not just the loudest or most confident people. It's about creating a space where people feel safe to share their ideas, concerns, and stories, knowing they won't be ignored. This isn't just about feeling good, it leads to fairness, sparks creativity, and helps teams and communities feel like they belong. When people know their input matters, they bring their best ideas, and that's when real innovation happens. There's a clear link between feeling safe and solving problems creatively; when people aren't afraid of being judged, they take more risks, share bold ideas, and find solutions that might otherwise stay hidden.

Even with good intentions, exclusion can happen through small habits. For example, in meetings, someone, often a woman or a colleague of color, might be interrupted, and their idea is later repeated by someone else and finally taken seriously. Sometimes it's more subtle: people talk over quieter voices or ignore comments from those outside the main group. These moments might seem small to some, but they add up and teach people it's safer to stay quiet. This hurts not just the individual, but the whole group, because you miss out on ideas that could make a big difference.

Building habits that make space for everyone starts with noticing who's getting airtime and who's being left out. One simple but powerful tool is the "talking stick." In person, you can literally pass an object around so only the person holding it speaks; online, features like the virtual hand-raise serve the same purpose. This slows down fast talkers and ensures turn-taking. If your group is larger or more prone to side chatter, appoint a facilitator to monitor who has spoken and who hasn't, gently. Their job isn't to police but to keep the conversation balanced, inviting those who haven't weighed in to share their thoughts.

Other strategies amplify voices that are often drowned out. If you notice someone's idea gets talked over or ignored, echo it back: "I want to go back to what Priya mentioned earlier, it sounded important." Sometimes all it takes is one person amplifying another's input to shift the group dynamic. If you're leading a meeting or discussion, set ground rules upfront, like a "no interruption" policy during brainstorming sessions or a five-second pause after someone finishes speaking before anyone else jumps in. This pause can feel awkward at first, but it gives quieter voices time to gather their thoughts and step forward.

Designing group norms that reinforce inclusion means making these practices part of your routine, not just one-off fixes. Consider feedback rounds at the end of meetings: everyone gets a chance to share what went well and what could be improved. According to a recent article in the field, breakout pairs create a space for participants who are less comfortable speaking in front of groups to share their thoughts with one person before joining a wider team conversation. Having rotating facilitators also helps keep discussions fresh and ensures leadership is not concentrated in a single person. In community organizations, "story circles" invite everyone to share a short experience on a theme before moving on; no commentary or debate until each story has been heard. These rituals aren't about forcing anyone to speak; they're about showing that every voice counts.

Regular "voice audits" can also change the game. Once a month or so, tally up who's been speaking in meetings or group settings. Are there patterns? Does one department dominate? Do women or marginalized colleagues rarely get the floor? Use this information as a nudge for self-correction. Maybe next time, intentionally invite those who've been quiet to start the conversation.

Quick Inclusive Listening Self-Check

After your next group discussion, jot down these questions:

- Who spoke the most? Who spoke least?

- Did anyone get interrupted, who and how often?

- Were any ideas repeated by different people? Who got credit?

- Did all perspectives get space, or did some voices fade into the background?

Reflect on your own role. Did you amplify others or dominate? Next time, aim to create space for at least one person who hasn't shared yet. Making this a habit turns inclusive listening from an aspiration into an everyday reality.

The true power of inclusive listening shows itself when people who usually hang back begin to step forward, knowing they'll be met with attention and respect. Voices multiply, and conversations deepen. You can feel the energy shift, the room gets brighter, ideas fly faster, and real trust grows stronger with each round of honest sharing.

What to Do When You Get It Wrong

Misunderstandings are bound to happen, especially when you're juggling different backgrounds, roles, or ways of expressing yourself. No matter how much you care, sometimes you'll miss a cue, read something the wrong way, or just plain mess up. The truth is, nobody listens perfectly all the time, not me, not you, not anyone. What you do after you misread someone matters most. The willingness to repair a misstep is the real glue that holds relationships together across all kinds of differences.

It's easy to feel defensive when you realize you misunderstood someone, maybe you cut them off, jumped to a conclusion, or made an assumption that didn't land well. The urge to explain yourself or downplay what happened can get strong. But growth comes from humility, not from always being right. When you own up to getting it wrong, you show you value the relationship more than your own comfort. A simple, "I realize I may have misread your meaning, can I clarify?" goes a long way. No need for a big production; just be honest and let the other person know you want to understand better.

Sometimes it's as straightforward as saying, "I'm sorry for interrupting; I want to make sure I understand your perspective." That short pause can shift the whole mood of the conversation. You're not making excuses or shifting blame; you're opening the door for real connection. If you sense tension or confusion after you've spoken, ask directly: "Would you be willing to share how I can listen better next time?" This kind of question builds trust and signals that feedback is welcome, not dangerous.

Repairing misreads isn't just about mending fences in the moment; it's about building habits that support long-term learning. Reopening a conversation might feel awkward, but it's often the only way to clear the air. You could say, "I've been thinking about our last talk, I'm worried I didn't fully get what you were trying to say. Can we revisit that?" Or, "Looking back, I realize I jumped in too soon. Is there anything I missed that you want me to hear?" These small invitations help others feel safe speaking their minds and sharing honestly.

Feedback is a two-way street. If someone tells you how your listening impacted them, resist the temptation to defend yourself immediately. Instead, try: "Thank you for letting me know. I appreciate your honesty." Sometimes feedback stings, but remember it's part of growing stronger as a listener, and as a person who wants real connection, not just surface-level harmony.

Reflection is where real progress happens. After a miscommunication, carve out time, even ten minutes, to think through what happened without judgment. Ask yourself: "What did I learn from this miscommunication?" Write it down if that helps. What signs did I miss? Was I rushing, distracted, or bringing my own baggage? These answers can be surprisingly eye-opening and provide clues for next time.

Teams and groups benefit from this kind of reflection, too. After finishing a project with people from different backgrounds or departments, set aside time for a debrief. Go beyond talking about outcomes, discuss how the communication flowed (or didn't). Questions like "Where did we misunderstand each other?" or "What would help us listen better as a group?" open the door to improvement. You don't need a formal process; even an informal chat over coffee can uncover new insights.

Role-playing is another underrated tool for building confidence in tricky conversations. Practice with a trusted friend or colleague, take turns acting out misunderstandings, and then repairing them. It feels awkward at first, but it quickly reveals blind spots and builds resilience for real-life situations.

Don't let mistakes turn into shame spirals or avoidance. Instead, treat each misstep as a signal, a nudge toward deeper understanding and stronger relationships. The more comfortable you get with repair, the less afraid you'll be of slipping up in the first place. This mindset, seeing mistakes as normal and fixable, frees everyone up to experiment, learn, and actually talk about what matters.

Wrapping up this chapter, remember that listening well isn't about never messing up; it's about owning your impact and being willing to try again. Repairing misreads builds bridges that last and turns awkward moments into opportunities for trust and growth. As we move forward, we'll look at how these skills come to life in digital spaces and virtual conversations, where misunderstandings can multiply fast but so can moments of true connection.

Chapter Eight

High-Stakes and Difficult Conversations

De-Escalation Tools for Heated Moments

Imagine a late-night argument in the kitchen, a partner's voice getting louder about an unpaid bill, or a harsh email from a coworker. The tension fills the room, your heart races, your face feels hot, and your fists clench. Anger doesn't slip in quietly; it takes over, pushing aside logic and making words come out wrong.

Anger isn't only a feeling; it shows up in your body. Recognizing these early signs can help you feel more in control and confident in guiding the conversation before it gets out of hand. Paying attention allows you to adjust and keep things on track.

Anger can be contagious. If you notice someone's voice getting sharper or their body tensing up, your own body might react too. That's a sign to slow things down. Listen on purpose: speak more slowly, use a softer tone, and lower your volume. This isn't about giving in; it's about changing the pace so everyone has space to think and respond. Often, just speaking a little more slowly and quietly can help calm things down.

How you carry yourself matters too. If things feel tense, give some space, lean back, step away for a moment, or suggest a short break: "Let's pause for a minute so we don't say anything we'll regret." Even a quick break or getting a glass of water can help everyone reset.

When you respond, try not to get defensive or sarcastic. Instead, acknowledge what you notice: "I can tell this really matters to you, let's take a breath and talk it through." Or, "I want to understand what's making you upset." These responses show you respect their feelings and help rebuild trust, reminding you both that this is a conversation, not a competition. Focus on understanding and repairing the relationship.

Spotting Your Anger Cues

Think about what anger feels like for you: maybe sweaty hands, a shaky voice, or a clenched jaw. Write down three physical signs you notice when you're upset. When you spot one of these in yourself or someone else, try to reset by slowing your speech, repeating what you've heard, or suggesting a quick break ("Let's take a breather for five minutes"). Notice how these small changes can shift the mood.

Stories make this clearer. Picture a manager whose upset employee storms in after a tough call. Instead of raising her voice or quoting rules, the manager calmly says, "You're frustrated because you feel no one's hearing the system's problems?" That simple acknowledgment helps the employee's anger fade, opening the door to solving the problem instead of more arguing.

Or imagine a parent and teen arguing about curfew. The teen says, "You never trust me! You want to control everything!" Instead of reacting emotionally, the parent calmly replies, "I get why this feels unfair. Can you help me understand what's bothering you about tonight?" The tension might not disappear, but now a real conversation can happen.

Listening through anger means staying present, even when you feel like defending yourself or arguing. Often, anger hides deeper feelings like stress, fear, or caring. By listening on purpose and noticing words, tone, and body language, both people can break out of the anger cycle. You don't have to give up your own boundaries. The goal is to be curious and try to understand, not to control the other person.

Everyone feels anger sometimes. But if you notice the early signs and listen carefully, you can turn tense conversations into real opportunities for connection and change.

How to Stay Curious When You Disapprove

You've likely been close to disconnecting during a heated debate, maybe about politics at a barbecue, healthcare on a family Zoom call, or a project disagreement at work. When we disagree, our bodies tense up, our minds race, and we want to argue or leave. But staying curious can help you stay connected and find common ground, even when you don't agree. You can stay grounded and connected by staying curious, even when you don't agree.

One helpful approach to handle disagreements is: Listen, Acknowledge, Explore, Express. It's not a cure-all, but it helps you stay engaged and respectful. First, really listen, don't plan your comeback, pay attention to their words, tone, and gestures. Try to understand what matters to them, even if you disagree. Next, acknowledge what you've heard by repeating their main points or feelings without sarcasm or judgment. For example, "It sounds like this issue is really important to you," or "I see you've thought about this a lot." People are more likely to open up when they feel truly heard and respected.

Next, explore their perspective. Curiosity is important here. Instead of asking, "Why would you think that?", which can sound harsh, invite them to share: "Can you tell me what led you to that view?" or "What experiences shaped your opinion?" You could also ask, "What's most important to you about this?" or "Which part matters most?" These questions move the conversation from arguing to understanding, focusing on beliefs and values instead of just taking sides. The goal isn't to gather points for a comeback, but to learn where the other person is coming from.

Finally, share your own view clearly and honestly, without blaming or acting superior. Use "I" statements and show respect: "I see this differently, but I want to understand how you got there," or, "I grew up in a different environment, so I see it another way." This keeps the conversation open and avoids personal criticism.

Here are some real-life examples. Two friends meet for coffee; one is worried about climate change, the other doubts government policies work. Instead of arguing, the first friend says, "I know we don't agree, but I'd like to understand your perspective. What makes you skeptical?" The other, surprised but not defensive, shares a story about growing up in a family business affected by regulations. Now, the conversation is about personal experience, not a shouting match. No one's mind changes right away, but both feel respected.

Or picture two coworkers disagreeing about a new project tool: one is excited for the new software, the other is worried about the change. Using this approach, one says, "I get that change is stressful. What's worked for you before? What worries you most?" The other shares concerns about training time and past tech problems. They realize they both want to work efficiently and start brainstorming how to make the rollout smoother.

Family disagreements can be even tougher. Siblings arguing about care decisions for an aging parent can quickly become resentful. Instead, asking questions like "What's behind your view?" or "Which part is most important to you?" helps everyone be honest about feelings like guilt, love, or fear, things that often get missed in surface-level arguments.

Curiosity is key: if you see disagreement as a chance to learn, not just to be right, you can stay connected even when you don't share the same values. It takes practice and patience; sometimes you'll have to hold back or sit with discomfort when you disagree. But choosing to understand instead of trying to "win" turns tense moments into real conversations and helps everyone feel heard.

To practice, try writing down your thoughts after difficult conversations. Ask yourself: Did I really listen? Did I acknowledge their point of view? What did I learn by being curious? Did I share my side without blaming? Over time, this helps you get better and turns disagreement into a chance to connect, not something to fear.

Listening to Feedback, Staying Open, Not Defensive

Getting feedback, especially when it hurts, can bring up strong emotions. You might feel embarrassed, defensive, or even angry, and it's easy to start making excuses or ignoring the feedback. This reaction is normal; almost everyone wants to defend themselves, even when they know feedback can help them grow. The important thing is to pause and notice this reflex before it takes over the conversation.

It helps to remind yourself: "This is about growth, not my worth." Separating who you are from what you do keeps shame away and encourages curiosity. Telling yourself, "Feedback isn't a judgment on me, it's information to help me improve," can make a big difference, even if the feedback is awkward or not well delivered. There's usually something useful in it.

How you react in the moment matters. Instead of shutting down or making excuses, keep your body language open: uncross your arms, nod, and make eye contact. Simple phrases like "I appreciate you sharing this," show you're listening, even if you feel unsettled. If the feedback is unclear, ask for more details calmly, such as, "Can you tell me more about what you noticed?" or "Could you share an example?" These questions turn vague feedback into clear steps and make it easier to know what's expected.

Sometimes, feedback is general: "You could communicate better in meetings." Gently ask for more detail: "What might improvement look like here?" or "Is there a recent example?" These questions help you avoid guessing and turn criticism into clear actions.

Taking a short pause before you respond is very helpful. Count to five in your head or take a slow breath to process what was said. If you're not sure you understand, repeat back what you heard: "Let me make sure I understand you before I respond." Restating their words helps clarify the feedback and shows respect, which can slow things down and ease tension.

After the conversation, reflect instead of replaying every detail or focusing on what felt unfair. Write down what stood out, any triggers, or patterns, like always feeling defensive with certain topics or people. Sometimes, you'll notice new insights once your emotions have settled.

You don't have to agree with or respond to feedback right away. It's okay to say, "I'd like to think about this and get back to you." Asking for time to process shows maturity. Later, you can return to the conversation: "I've been thinking about our talk. Can we discuss ways I can work on this skill?" Treating feedback as a team effort turns it into a partnership rather than just criticism.

Applying Feedback in Different Settings

Consider a teacher hearing a parent's concerns about classroom management. Instead of explaining away the worry, the teacher asks, "Could you describe what your child said?" This leads to a more productive conversation and practical solutions for both sides. Or picture a team lead in a performance review. Rather than making excuses, she says, "I want to grow. Can you give an example of how I might approach project updates differently?" This encourages her manager to provide support.

At home, listening to feedback can defuse tension. If a partner feels overwhelmed by household tasks, instead of defending past efforts, you might ask, "What would help lighten your load?" This simple question moves from frustration to collaborative problem-solving.

Feedback almost always stings at first; most people feel uncomfortable or embarrassed. But if you see it as a tool for growth and respond with openness and curiosity, it gets easier and builds trust and self-awareness.

Using simple phrases, reflecting, and staying curious help you learn and grow, turning tough conversations into real progress. Over time, these small changes turn hard feedback into chances to improve and build stronger relationships.

Apologies That Land, Listening as the First Step in Repair

A real apology isn't found in a quick "I'm sorry," but in how you show up and listen before saying anything. When your actions hurt someone, the urge to explain or defend yourself is natural, but it rarely helps. The best apologies begin with quiet presence: sit with the person, let them speak, and listen without interrupting or fidgeting. Give them the space to feel truly seen and heard; this matters more than your first words.

After listening, reflect on what you've heard before you respond. Recognize their pain, their words, and their body language, without preparing your defense or response. Absorb how your actions affected them. When it's time to apologize, start by naming exactly what you did and how it impacted them: "I hear how my actions hurt you..." Acknowledging their pain directly, without offering your perspective, does more for rebuilding trust than explanations ever could. Thank them for telling you, especially if it was hard: "Thank you for telling me. How can I make this right?" Let their needs guide your next steps, not your wish for quick forgiveness.

Many apologies fail because they rush to "sorry" or focus on your discomfort. Rushing past their pain or minimizing it with phrases like "It wasn't that bad," or centering yourself ("I'm sorry you feel that way") shifts the focus away from your responsibility. These traps show that your priority is to move on or ease your guilt, not to help them heal. Instead, keep your focus on their experience. If you catch yourself leaning toward excuses, "I didn't mean to..." or "You misunderstood", pause and redirect. The most healing apologies take full ownership: "I'm sorry for what I did," not "I'm sorry if you were offended."

Effective apologies are specific and paired with action. For example, at work, if you snapped at a colleague, wait until emotions cool, then approach them privately, not with excuses, but with honesty: "I spoke sharply to you earlier, and that was unkind. I hear how it made you feel dismissed; I'm sorry for that. What can I do to set things right?" The formula is simple: listen first, own your mistake, then ask how to repair. This approach can turn resentment into renewed respect.

In friendships, broken trust often feels even heavier. If you forgot to support a friend at an important event, don't hide behind texts or make excuses. Reach out directly, ask to talk, and let them share how your absence felt. Then apologize: "It sounds like my not showing up made you feel unimportant. I can see why that hurt." Ask, "Is there anything I can do to rebuild our friendship?" Sometimes, all it takes is a genuine conversation; sometimes, time is needed.

Family apologies can be the hardest but also most meaningful. For example, a parent who lost their temper might later sit quietly with their child and say, "You looked scared when I raised my voice, and I'm sorry for yelling. You didn't deserve that." Even if the child can't fully express their feelings, this plants seeds of trust and safety.

Asking "How can I make it right?" is an act of humility in a sincere apology. Sometimes, people know what they need: a redo, time, or simply reassurance that you mean to do better. Other times, they want to know you're listening and that their feelings matter.

Listening is the foundation of real repair. Without it, even a well-worded apology rings hollow. When you slow down to hear the full story of someone's hurt and accept the weight of your impact, your apology reaches not just their ears, but their heart. That's when trust can begin to rebuild, one honest conversation at a time.

Recovering a Conversation, Resetting After a Misstep

You know that feeling when a conversation takes a sharp turn, and suddenly you're both off in the weeds? Maybe you realize you've jumped to conclusions, or you cut someone off mid-thought, or maybe an emotional trigger took over, and now the mood in the room is tense. It's like driving and missing your exit. Now, everyone's annoyed, and you're not even sure where you're headed. Recognizing this moment is half the battle. When you sense that things have derailed, maybe there's confusion, raised voices, or just an awkward silence, it's a clear sign to stop and reassess before pushing forward. The key is not to wait until resentment simmers or people shut down. You can call a reset in real time, and it changes everything.

Pausing a conversation doesn't have to feel dramatic or loaded with blame. You can keep it light and constructive. Language matters here. Instead of pushing on, try, "I think we've gotten off track, can we start over?" That simple line shifts the dynamic from adversarial to collaborative. Or if you realize you made an assumption, call it out: "I just realized I was guessing what you meant, and I might be off base." This kind of honesty is disarming. It signals respect for the other person's perspective and gives everyone space to breathe. You don't have to make it a big deal; acknowledge what happened and invite a fresh start.

After calling a reset, it helps to revisit the reason for talking in the first place. Ask out loud, "What do we want to get out of this conversation?" Bringing the focus back to the shared goal reminds everyone why you're there. It turns the spotlight from who's "right" to what matters most. This question works wonders in almost any situation, at work, at home, or in group chats that go sideways.

In more formal settings, like a team meeting gone sideways after a confusing update, don't be afraid to hit pause. You might say, "It seems like we're talking past each other. Let's take a step back. What are we actually trying to solve here?" Openly acknowledging confusion can feel risky, but it usually leads to relief. People want clarity and direction. Often, team members will chime in with their perspectives on the issue, and together you can build a clear path forward.

Resetting in personal conversations can be trickier because emotions run higher and old patterns surface quickly. Imagine a couple in the middle of a heated debate about chores. One partner snaps, "You never help around here," and the other retorts, "That's not fair!" Instead of letting it spiral, one person says, "I think I got defensive just now. Can we pause and try again?" That openness breaks the cycle of blame and creates room for real listening. Or take siblings arguing over text about family plans, if the thread starts getting snippy, try, "Wait, I think I'm misunderstanding you. Can we clarify what each of us wants out of this weekend?" These small interventions can save hours of back-and-forth resentment.

The reset works just as well in digital as in face-to-face conversations. If you sense tone getting lost or assumptions piling up in an email or group chat, it helps to say something like, "I'm realizing this thread is getting confusing, can we hop on a quick call or clarify what we're hoping to decide?" This stops the escalation that so often happens with written words.

It takes courage to stop and call for a reset instead of bulldozing through awkwardness or pretending nothing happened. But being willing to admit when things have gone off track is a strength, not a weakness. You model humility and make it safe for others to do the same. The more you practice these resets, the more natural they become, and the less time you spend untangling hurt feelings later.

What ties all these resets together is an attitude of curiosity and care. You're not pointing fingers or keeping score; you're inviting everyone, including yourself, to refocus on what matters. Conversation resets are not about erasing conflict or pretending mistakes didn't happen. They're about acknowledging human messiness and choosing clarity over confusion.

Finishing up this chapter, remember that every conversation, even tough ones, offers another chance to build trust if you're willing to notice when things veer off course and gently steer them back. Resetting isn't just about cleaning up messes; it's about valuing connection over being right. Up next: we'll look at how these listening skills translate into building habits that last and ripple outward into your relationships, teams, and communities.

Chapter Nine

Listening in the Digital Age

Tackling Zoom Fatigue, Staying Engaged on Video Calls

It can feel like the days of meeting around a conference table and picking up on in-person cues are long gone. Now, both work and home life often mean jumping from one video call to another, staring at faces in little boxes, and trying to look engaged even as you get tired. Maybe you catch yourself zoning out, sneaking a look at your phone, or watching your own video more than the person speaking. Tools like Zoom, Teams, and Meet are now part of daily life, each with its own challenges for good listening.

"Zoom fatigue" is more than just a buzzword. Research shows that people feel more tired and less focused after video meetings than after in-person meetings (see APA list #6). It's not just about staring at a screen. On video calls, your brain has to work harder to read facial expressions, voice tones, and body language, all while you keep an eye on how you look. This kind of multitasking quickly uses up your mental energy. Technical problems, audio delays, and constant interruptions make things even harder, often leaving you exhausted even though you haven't left your chair.

All this digital overload makes it harder to listen well. If you're worried about your background or how you look, it's easy to miss the main idea, forget details, or stop feeling empathy for others who also seem tired. Recognizing these feelings helps you connect better and feel more compassionate during meetings. With every new meeting link, it can feel like the emotional connection fades a bit more. If you end your day feeling cranky, foggy, tense, or with sore eyes or a headache, you're probably dealing with "screen fatigue." Feeling irritable, impatient, or wanting to disconnect from others are common mental signs, too.

So how do you stay engaged and really listen during video calls? Start with the basics: treat important meetings as if you were there in person. Try turning your camera on and turning off notifications, especially when the meeting matters or you're leading. Showing your reactions, even if your background or hair isn't perfect, helps bring back some human connection. Turning off pop-ups and alerts also helps you stay focused.

Try not to get stuck in back-to-back video calls. Schedule short breaks, even just five minutes, between meetings to stretch, walk around, and rest your eyes. For less important updates or routine check-ins, make it okay to turn the camera off. This gives everyone a break and helps ease the pressure of always being on screen.

Pay attention to when you or others start to lose focus, look away, doodle, or seem distracted. If that happens, take a quick break so everyone can stretch or do a fast "one-word check-in" about how they're feeling. If the group seems tired, it's okay to turn off cameras for a bit or switch to a phone call.

Camera rules can be tough to figure out. Don't feel like you or others have to keep cameras on if it's making people tired. Discuss with your team setting clear expectations, such as having cameras on for the first 15 minutes and then turning them off, to balance connection with well-being.

Meeting facilitators help build trust and keep people engaged. Try starting with a "check-in round" where everyone shares how they're feeling, without talking about work. This simple habit encourages openness and makes team members feel valued. It also sets a positive tone, helping everyone be more receptive and ready to listen.

Don't let one person run the meeting all the time. Take turns being the facilitator so everyone shares the responsibility. Use quick polls or reaction emojis to check how people are feeling and to help quieter team members share their thoughts or ask questions early on. This approach makes everyone feel involved and respected, fostering a more inclusive environment.

Are You Really Listening on Zoom?

- Are you distracted by other tabs or devices?

- Do you remember discussion points from five minutes ago?

- Are you tempted to multitask or claim "technical issues"

- What's your body telling you, tension, restlessness?

If you notice you're losing focus, try a quick reset. Close any distractions, stand up for a moment, or type a comment in the chat to get back into the conversation.

Digital meetings aren't going anywhere, but small changes, like using your camera on purpose, taking breaks, checking in with yourself, and making sure everyone can speak, can turn video calls from tiring tasks into real chances for connection and better listening.

Listening Well in Text, Slack, Email, and Group Chats

Reading and replying to lots of messages isn't just about staying up to date; it's a form of listening that's easy to overlook. Tools like Slack, email, and group chats have changed how we communicate. You can't rely on a raised eyebrow or a smile to figure out someone's mood anymore. Now, you're left guessing at words that might not give you all the clues you need. Because there's a delay between sending and getting a reply, you might fill in the blanks yourself, sometimes assuming the worst if someone replies late or in a different tone. Without tone or body language, even a simple "okay" can sound cold. If you've ever stared at a Slack message and wondered, "Are they upset? Did I do something wrong?" you know how tricky this can be.

This kind of confusion is part of written communication. Your brain works extra hard to find context that might not be there. It's easy to misread sarcasm or urgency, and even simple messages can make you anxious if you're not careful. You might start to overthink things, a slow reply feels like rejection, a short answer seems like disapproval, or a really excited reply looks unprofessional. The reality is that text-based tools make misunderstandings more likely and leave plenty of room for guessing.

To avoid confusion, I follow a simple rule before replying to any message that bothers me: "Read twice, react once." First, I read the words. Then I look for context: what's happening in the conversation, the sender's usual style, and whether there's a deadline. Only after that do I decide how to respond. Taking this pause can help save relationships, projects, and your own peace of mind. If a message still feels strange, remember the sender might just be distracted, busy, or dealing with something else.

You can pick up extra clues by noticing when and how people message. Is someone who's usually chatty now being brief? Are they replying late at night? Do they use lots of exclamation marks or keep things short? These details matter. Context adds meaning to plain text. Instead of jumping to conclusions, think about what else might be going on for them.

Good written communication means showing you're paying attention, even if you can't see the other person. Paraphrasing works on Slack just like it does in person. For example, you might say, "Just to clarify, you're saying we should move the deadline to Friday?" This lets both sides confirm or correct things quickly. Summarizing long threads also helps everyone stay on track: "To recap, Sam will handle the report, and I'll schedule a client review for next week." These habits make things clearer and help projects move forward.

Don't forget how helpful a quick reply can be. Even if you don't have all the answers, send a short message like, "Received, let me look into this and get back to you by the end of the day." This small step shows respect and helps keep everyone calm. In group chats, tag people directly when you need their input ("@Jordan, can you weigh in on this?") so nothing gets missed.

It's important to write clearly and include everyone, especially since people might be busy or using different languages. Avoid using jargon or inside jokes unless you know everyone understands. When giving feedback or making requests, be direct but polite. For example, "Could you review this by noon?" is better than being vague or unclear.

Group emails can easily get out of hand with too many replies. Before you hit send, ask yourself if everyone really needs to see your message. Use "reply all" only when necessary, and move off-topic chats or side conversations to private messages. This helps keep inboxes under control and reduces digital clutter.

Setting clear chat rules helps everyone know what to expect. Decide as a group which channels are for important decisions and which are for casual talk. For example, "Let's use #team-decisions for urgent things and #random for jokes or weekend plans." This way, important info doesn't get lost among memes or birthday messages.

Sometimes, things still get tense over text. If you notice this happening, don't let it build up. Ask kindly, "Just checking, was my last message clear? Is there anything I can explain?" Making space for questions helps keep things smooth and avoids misunderstandings.

The digital world has changed how we listen, but everyone still wants to feel heard and understood. Small changes in how you read and reply can make text conversations friendlier, clearer, and much less stressful for everyone.

Emoji, GIFs, and Tone: Reading Between the Digital Lines

If you've ever looked at a message full of emojis and weren't sure how to respond, you're not alone. Emojis, GIFs, and memes are like their own language. They can help when words aren't enough, but sometimes they also cause confusion or misunderstandings.

Emojis are a fast way to show how you feel, but they can be tricky. A thumbs-up might mean "I got it" to one person but seem rude or dismissive to someone else. Different groups and ages use emojis in their own ways. For example, younger people use the skull emoji to mean something is really funny ("I'm dead"), while older people might think it means something is wrong. Even a simple smiley face can come across as friendly or sarcastic, depending on who sends it and the situation. In the end, what one person means as cheerful, another might see as a complaint. Context matters most.

GIFs and memes add fun and personality to chats. They can make tense moments lighter, show appreciation, or make group conversations more lively. Sometimes a meme says "I get it" better than words ever could. But if someone doesn't get the joke or reference, it can feel confusing or leave them out. For example, a playful eye roll GIF might make one person laugh but confuse or upset someone else. The right meme brings people together, but the wrong one can make someone feel left out.

There's also the "..." typing indicator, which can make people feel all sorts of things. Seeing those dots can make you wonder if a compliment, a complaint, or just a lunch invite is coming. The longer the dots stay, the more anxious you might feel. If the message never comes, you might even worry about your relationship. It's surprising how much meaning those three dots can have.

Reading digital communication requires a bit of detective work. Before reacting to an emoji or meme, consider your relationship with the sender, your usual back-and-forth, and the context. Are you joking or dealing with something serious? If confused, don't dwell on it; ask. A quick "Did you mean that as a joke?" or "We're still good, right?" clears things up and saves needless worry.

To use emojis and GIFs in a caring way, match them to the situation. Sending a heart or hug emoji when someone shares bad news shows support without making things heavier. For good news, a confetti emoji or a fun GIF can add to the excitement. Humor helps too; a funny animal video or meme can ease tension after a disagreement and show you're still on good terms.

But it's important not to overdo it. Using too many emojis can make them less meaningful and might bother people who prefer more direct messages. Adjust your tone to the person you're talking to and the situation, especially at work. In new or mixed groups, stick to simple emojis like thumbs-ups or clapping hands until you know what works. As you get to know people, you can use more playful ones.

Misunderstandings online are bound to happen. If you think someone took an emoji or GIF the wrong way, say so and clear it up quickly. For example, you could write, "Sorry, that GIF was meant to cheer you up, not make light of your concern." If a chat feels tense, check in directly: "Hey, did my last message make sense?" Most people appreciate it and will explain if needed.

Your Emoji & GIF Decoder

Think about the emoji or GIF you used most this week. What did you want it to say? Now ask a friend or coworker what it means to them. Compare what you meant with how they see it. This simple check-in helps you understand yourself and close communication gaps online.

Digital symbols will keep changing, but if you stay curious and pay attention to what they mean for you and others, your communication will stay clear and real.

Preventing Digital Misunderstandings, Setting Norms and Boundaries

Few things are more confusing or frustrating than a digital message that gets misunderstood or ignored. Online, there's little room for error; a single missed email can make people question your priorities, respect, or even your friendship. Maybe you send a message, wait, and then wonder if you're being ignored or misunderstood. A friendly reminder can come across as demanding, and a harmless joke might sound like criticism. These mix-ups are common. Timing matters too; a slow reply can make you anxious, especially if you expect quick answers. If someone stops replying altogether ("ghosting"), you might feel unimportant or invisible. On top of that, too many messages, notifications, and "urgent" requests can be overwhelming. If you've ever dreaded checking your inbox, you know what this feels like.

Misunderstanding what's urgent is another problem. A quick "can we talk now?" might make someone think there's an emergency, and a message in all caps can feel like shouting. Even late-night messages, meant as simple reminders, can make people feel they have to reply right away. Over time, these things can hurt trust and make real communication harder.

The best way to avoid these problems is to set clear expectations with your team, family, or friends. Don't leave everyone guessing; discuss what's normal. Maybe agree urgent messages require a response within two hours, while non-urgent ones can wait a day. This eliminates second-guessing and reduces stress. If you work unconventional hours or across time zones, clarify: "I send late-night emails so I don't forget, but reply when you're online." For group chats, agree on response windows: "If it's about tonight's dinner, reply by 5 p.m.; non-urgent things can wait." These small agreements help everyone feel considered and respected.

Setting digital boundaries is important. Protecting your focus and emotional energy isn't selfish; it's necessary. Use status indicators like "In Focus Mode" or "Do Not Disturb." If you can, add a custom message to show when you need quiet or when you'll be available, like "Unavailable, will answer after 2." In groups, set up "no message" times after work or on weekends. For example, "No work texts after 7 p.m. except for emergencies," or "Sundays are for family, save work until Monday." Respecting these boundaries helps everyone recharge and avoids resentment.

Boundaries only work if everyone respects them, and that means having open conversations. If someone keeps messaging after hours or expects quick replies when you're off, bring it up kindly but clearly: "I've noticed we've had a few after-hours messages lately. Can we talk about how to handle those? I need some offline time to recharge." If your own message goes unanswered and it bothers you, check in gently: "I noticed my last note didn't get a reply, was the timing off? Should I resend?" These check-ins help stop small misunderstandings from turning into bigger issues.

It also helps to agree on what counts as "urgent." What's urgent for one person might be routine for someone else. Decide together what really needs a quick response, and use clear subject lines or tags like "[Urgent]" or "[FYI]" so people can prioritize calmly. In families, maybe only "locked out" or "emergency trip to the vet" is urgent; everything else can wait. At work, clear labels help everyone sort messages sensibly.

You can't avoid all digital misunderstandings, but they're easier to handle when you have clear rules and boundaries. If someone crosses a boundary, sends too many messages during your downtime, or ignores an important thread, talk about it clearly and kindly. You might say, "Hey, I try to avoid weekend messages unless it's urgent, can we stick to that?" Or after sending too many messages: "Sorry for all the pings earlier, I'll group updates next time to keep it easier."

Setting and keeping healthy digital rules isn't just about being efficient; it's about building trust and respect. When everyone knows what to expect, there's less stress and more real connection, both online and in person.

Building Your Connection Remotely, Mini Rituals for Virtual Teams

Moving to online meetings has taken away the casual moments that once brought teams and families together. Chatting in the kitchen or catching up in the hallway helped build trust and friendships. Without these natural interactions, digital teams can start to feel distant or disconnected. Now, building a connection takes effort; it won't just happen on its own.

Intentional rituals can help fill this gap and turn digital routines into real connections. Some teams start meetings with a "rose, thorn, bud" check-in: everyone shares something good (rose), a challenge (thorn), and something new they're looking forward to (bud). This goes beyond small talk and lets people be open and even laugh together, making everyone feel noticed. These rituals break down barriers, especially when managers and new hires share their hopes and struggles. Over time, regular check-ins help people feel safe speaking up and listening more closely.

Another good idea is to set up virtual coffee chats or "random buddy calls." Instead of waiting for chance meetings, teams can schedule regular pairings so everyone gets to talk with someone new each week. The chat can be about anything except work, or you can use a prompt like, "Share one thing you wish others knew about your job." These one-on-one chats bring back the casual hallway feel and help quieter people speak up. Families can use this too; siblings might have virtual breakfasts or movie nights to stay close across time zones.

Some groups make online connections more fun. One team uses themed Zoom backgrounds every Friday, like tropical islands, superheroes, or childhood photos. Others create shared playlists where everyone adds songs that match their mood or celebrate big moments, like finishing a project. Some group chats have "meme-of-the-week" contests or give shout-outs for small wins, building inside jokes and shared memories that make remote life feel less lonely.

Create rituals that fit your group's style and needs. Ask for ideas, send a poll like, "What would help us feel more connected?" and let people suggest check-in questions, themes, or times for social calls. Take turns choosing the ritual to keep things fresh and fair. One week could be a gratitude round, another could be "two truths and a lie." After a month, check in as a group to see what's working and what feels forced, and adjust until the rituals feel natural, not just another task.

To start, try a single ritual at your next meeting or group chat. Some people may be skeptical, but stick with it; a few cycles usually win people over once they see genuine benefits. Consistency and openness to feedback are key; no ritual is perfect from the start.

These digital rituals aren't just for work. Families use shared photo albums or Sunday "virtual dinners" to stay close. Friends organize online game nights or themed happy hours to keep laughter alive. Regardless of the group, the principle is the same: create intentional spaces for connection so relationships don't fade behind screens.

As you try mini-rituals, remember they work best when everyone helps shape them. The more voices in the process, the more likely rituals are to resonate. Keep the tone light, personal, and open to change. Rituals should feel like a welcome break, not another chore.

Remote life doesn't have to mean shallow connections or loneliness. With a little creativity and effort, you can nurture trust and a sense of belonging across distance. Small acts, checking in, sharing playlists, laughing together, create lasting bonds, even when you're miles apart.

A Simple Rituals Checklist

- Try "rose, thorn, bud" at your next meeting or family call.

- Set up rotating virtual coffee chats with coworkers or friends.

- Experiment with weekly themes, Zoom backgrounds, memes, and playlists.

- Survey the group after four weeks: keep what works, adjust what doesn't.

- Rotate who sets the ritual each week or month for fairness and variety.

Connection in digital spaces takes intentionality, but it's absolutely possible. The rituals you start now will shape your team's trust tomorrow. Next, we'll dig into how to make listening skills stick as daily habits, wherever and however you connect.

Chapter Ten

Building Habits and a Listening Culture

Micro-Habits for Everyday Listening, Making Change Stick

After a long day, you might catch yourself nodding at your partner while thinking about work emails, or heading into a team meeting already planning how to wrap up fast. Building small, repeatable habits like brushing your teeth or locking your door shows you can make meaningful change without overnight effort, making you feel capable and motivated.

Let's be honest: Real change often comes from small steps rather than big promises. While research such as Nie, Fu, Rehman, and Zaigham's 2022 study shows incidental vocabulary learning through listening, it also highlights how micro-habits can subtly improve listening over time.

For example, before each meeting, silence your phone, not just turning it face down, but actually muting notifications so nothing interrupts the speaker. This only takes a few seconds but tells your brain, and those around you, that it's time to listen. Doing this regularly makes it automatic. Soon, you won't even think about it; you'll do it. Your mind learns that this is listening time.

Another helpful micro-habit is to take a single deep breath before answering any question. It might seem small, but that quick pause gives you a moment to think, check your reaction, and respond more thoughtfully. Even one second of stillness can improve your answers and help you stay calm in conversation.

Micro-habits are flexible. Think of them like a menu, choose what fits your life, style, or even your mood that day. For example, you could end every conversation by asking, "Is there anything else you'd like to share?" This question often helps people open up and creates a real connection, whether you're at work or just chatting in line at the store.

You could also set a daily "listening intention" when you start your morning. For example, while you have your first coffee or tea, take ten seconds to decide how you'll listen today, like, "I'll let my partner finish their story," or "I'll ask one clarifying question in today's meeting." Write it on a sticky note or repeat it to yourself. The goal isn't perfection; it's about moving a little closer to the listener you want to become.

If you want to focus on home life, try pausing for three seconds before replying to family members. In emotional or tough conversations, silently count to three before you answer. Those extra moments give space for deeper sharing and help prevent quick, automatic reactions. If counting isn't helpful, try linking your reply to a physical gesture, like touching your thumb and forefinger together, or changing your posture before you speak.

Some people find it easier to build habits by connecting them to routines they already have, a method called habit stacking. You probably already have set routines, like morning coffee, brushing your teeth, or commuting. Habit stacking means pairing a new action with these regular habits. For example, focus on active listening during your morning coffee with a family member or during a work check-in. Use this as your reminder to put away distractions and listen with intention.

Transitions are great times to start micro-habits. If you drive a child to school or commute with a coworker, let that be your "listening time." Ask, "What's on your mind this morning?" and focus on really listening instead of jumping in with advice. When you connect these habits to things you already do, they soon feel natural and don't seem like extra work.

Of course, building new habits isn't always easy. You might forget, lose motivation, or fall back into old routines, especially when you're busy or stressed. That's normal. Remember, the goal is progress, not perfection, and each step forward helps you feel supported and resilient.

It's common to forget. Prompts like sticky notes ("Pause before replying!"), calendar reminders ("Silence phone!"), Or a rubber band on your wrist serves as a cue to reinforce your micro-habits. Digital alerts, like phone notifications, can also remind you of your listening goals for the day.

Losing motivation, especially when progress seems slow, is another challenge. The answer is to give yourself small, regular rewards. Notice and mentally congratulate yourself each time you practice a micro-habit, even if it's just once ("Nice work"), or treat yourself after a week of sticking with it. Sharing these small wins with someone supportive can also make your progress feel more real.

Everyone slips up sometimes. Instead of being hard on yourself, see these moments as useful information. Ask yourself what got in the way. Were you tired, distracted, or in a hurry? Adjust your goal or routine as needed. Maybe make the habit smaller, like pausing for one second instead of three, or try it at a different time of day.

Micro-habits should be simple enough to fit into even the busiest days. Some people make eye contact when greeting others; others do a quick mental check, "Am I listening or just waiting to talk?", before a conversation. Over time, these small changes can make a big difference in how people experience you and how you experience them.

Your Micro-Habit Builder

Pick two micro-habits from the list below (or invent your own), and write them down somewhere visible for tomorrow:

- Silence notifications before meetings.

- Take one deep breath before answering.

- End conversations with "Is there anything else?"

- Set a daily listening intention.

- Pause three seconds before replying at home.

- Use commute time for intentional listening.

- Ask one open-ended question at lunch.

- Make eye contact during greetings.

- Touch thumb and forefinger together before tough talks.

- Check posture as someone starts speaking.

Connect each habit to something you already do, like morning coffee, preparing dinner, or work meetings. If you forget tomorrow, don't worry, try again next time.

Real change happens when you repeat small actions until they become part of who you are, not from making big gestures. When people around you start to feel more heard, you'll know your micro-habits are working.

Tracking Your Progress, Reflection, Journals, and Feedback Loops

When you first decide to become a better listener, the early days can feel exciting. You notice small wins and maybe even see people react with surprise when they feel heard. But like any new habit, that excitement fades as life gets busy and old routines take over. If you're not careful, your commitment to listening can slip into the background, just like unused gym memberships or forgotten hobbies. That's why tracking your progress is so important. When you record your efforts, you make invisible change visible, which helps you keep going even after the initial excitement fades.

Think of tracking as your anchor during tough times. On hard days, it's easy to wonder if you're really improving or just imagining it. Did you make a difference in that conversation, or did you miss the mark? According to research by Kim and Cha, keeping a regular notebook or digital document for listening practice can be just as effective as other methods, such as dictation, for improving listening skills. Just jot down moments, big or small, when you really listened. Maybe you paused for your teenager to vent, let a colleague finish their story, or noticed someone's body language change because you gave them your full attention. These notes become real proof that you're showing up differently, even if progress feels slow.

A notebook also helps you build momentum. It's satisfying to see the pages fill up with real examples of your new habits. On tough days, looking back at earlier entries can boost your motivation. You'll remember, "I did this before so that I can do it again. According to research by Stojanovic and colleagues, using apps to track habits can support the intentional formation of new study behaviors by helping users monitor their progress and stay motivated. Some people also find it helpful to color-code calendar entries on days they practice a new habit, which adds a sense of reward and accountability.

Reflection is where tracking really matters. It's not just about collecting gold stars or counting wins; it's about noticing patterns, setbacks, and surprises. Each evening, or whenever works for you, pick a prompt and write a few lines: "What was my best listening moment today?" This helps you see what's working and builds positive habits. Or try, "When did I struggle to stay present, and why?" You might notice it's always after a long commute or when emails pile up. Now you know what challenges your focus and what you can adjust.

Another helpful reflection is to ask yourself, "Who did I make feel truly heard this week?" We often focus on where we fell short, but taking time to notice whose day you improved by listening can change how you see yourself and your impact. This question reminds you that listening affects others and that its effects reach beyond just you.

Self-reflection is only part of the process. To grow even more, ask for feedback from people around you. You might be surprised by the insights a trusted friend or partner can offer. Try setting up a monthly "listening check-in", maybe over coffee with your partner or a colleague,and ask, "How listened-to did you feel this month?" You can use a simple 1 to 5 scale or just let them share. The goal isn't to defend yourself, but to learn and notice things you might miss on your own.

If asking for feedback feels intimidating, start small. After a specific conversation, ask, "Hey, during our last talk, did you feel like I was really present? Is there anything I could do differently next time?" These direct questions take courage but invite honest feedback you might not get otherwise. Over time, these feedback loops build trust, showing others you're serious about improving and that you value their experience.

Getting feedback in group settings can be eye-opening. At work, try using a quick "How listened-to did you feel?" scale after meetings, a sticky note on each desk, or a digital poll. At home, make space at Sunday dinner for everyone to share a time they felt truly listened to that week. These rituals not only track progress but also encourage more listening by making it visible and valued.

Trying out different tracking tools can make the process enjoyable instead of a chore. Some people like using sticky notes on the fridge for every listening win or a progress board where you move colored magnets each time you reach your goal. Families might keep a jar on the counter, adding a marble for each day someone felt especially heard. At work, visual progress boards or simple charts can track group participation. Did everyone get a chance to speak? Were all voices included? Color-coded dots or stickers give instant feedback and can even spark friendly competition.

If you prefer digital tools, habit-tracking apps aren't just for steps or water; they work well for listening goals, too. Set daily reminders like "Ask one open-ended question today," and check them off before bed. Some apps let you track streaks or send gentle reminders if you fall behind. If you use a calendar, try color-coding events where you practiced listening: green for "fully present," yellow for "partial effort," and red for "missed opportunity." Over time, you'll see patterns. Maybe Mondays go well, but Fridays need more attention.

Reflection questions can make your tracking routine more meaningful. Try rotating through prompts each week: What was my hardest listening challenge? When did I notice impatience? Who surprised me when I slowed down and listened? Which setting, home, work, or community, was easiest or hardest for me to listen well? What emotion most often distracts me? What helps me get back on track when I slip? These questions do more than fill journal pages; they reveal patterns that help you build better strategies over time.

Sometimes it's helpful to track not just what happened, but how you felt. After a day of intentional listening, write down one word to describe your mood before and after: anxious, calm, proud, or relieved. Over time, you'll probably notice that being present helps others and also changes how you feel, a reward that's easy to overlook when you're focused on results.

The real benefit of tracking is making your progress visible, especially when no one else is watching or cheering you on. When your motivation drops, and it will, those notes or colored calendar squares remind you that you're still growing, even if it's slow. They help you stay committed when outside rewards are hard to find.

You might also want to create a ritual for reflection. Maybe every Friday afternoon becomes your "listening review" time, a chance to look back at the week's wins and challenges and set a new intention for the next week. For some, sharing these insights with a trusted friend or your team makes the impact even bigger and helps keep everyone accountable.

Check in with yourself regularly: Is tracking helping you notice growth, or is it just making you anxious? If it starts to feel like a burden, make it simpler. Try recording just one win per day or reflecting once a week instead of every night.

Tracking isn't about being perfect or competing with others; it's about building awareness over time. The more notes you collect, whether in a notebook, app, feedback check-in, or on a visual board, the clearer your path forward becomes. Each note is a small celebration of your effort, each reflection shows you how to build stronger habits, and each bit of feedback reveals new ways to grow as a listener.

If you notice yourself drifting from your intentions, use your tracking system as a reset, not as a punishment, but as a reminder of why this matters. Listening well isn't about checking boxes; it's about building deeper connections and being present over time. Your progress might not be a straight line, but with awareness and reflection, every conversation helps you move forward.

Teaching and Modeling Listening In Teams, Families, and Communities

Changing your listening habits is a big step, but real transformation happens when others start doing the same. One person who truly listens can change the mood of a whole room; kids might stay longer at dinner, meetings feel less boring, and arguments cool down. This ripple effect doesn't come from giving lectures; it starts with your example, how you pay attention, ask questions, and show you're present when someone else is speaking.

Just modeling good listening is often more powerful than giving instructions. At home, closing your laptop or putting your phone away to focus on a family member says, "You matter now." In meetings or busy gatherings, making eye contact and leaning in shows you're present, and others usually follow your lead. People notice your full attention, even if they don't say anything; you can see the relief in their posture or voice. This listening spreads to others.

Your influence goes both ways. When you give someone your full attention at dinner, you set the mood for the whole evening. At work, taking time to really listen to a teammate can inspire others to do the same. You can encourage this change by sharing a favorite listening habit at a meeting or family gathering, like letting everyone take turns sharing something that made their day better or harder. It's not about being perfect; it's about being present and inviting others to join in.

Bringing listening rituals into group settings doesn't have to feel stiff or awkward; it can actually be fun. Try starting meetings with a "round of appreciations," where everyone shares something positive about someone else. It might sound cheesy, but you'll notice people relax and connect more easily. According to a study by Jerica M. Berge and colleagues, having a clear structure and positive interactions during family meals, such as setting simple conversation guidelines, can help make mealtimes more organized and meaningful for everyone involved. Gentle reminders and positive examples from adults can encourage these habits without strict enforcement.

Community groups can also benefit from listening rituals. For example, volunteer groups might use "listening circles," where only one person speaks at a time, and everyone else listens, no interruptions, advice, or solutions until everyone has had a turn. This helps the group slow down, build trust, and ensure all voices are heard.

If you want to encourage others to listen better, positive reinforcement is powerful. When you notice someone doing it, maybe by waiting out an awkward silence or asking a clarifying question, mention it: "I noticed how you really listened to Jane earlier; that was great." This feedback makes good listening more likely to happen again. You can also help the group reflect after big conversations or projects. Ask what worked well, what stalled communication, and what could improve next time. Keep the tone curious and low-pressure; the goal is to learn, not lay blame.

These practices are especially helpful for teams or families where conflict or miscommunication is an issue. Sometimes, just taking time to talk honestly about listening and what gets in the way makes a huge difference. Debriefing after a tough moment helps everyone see that listening isn't about being flawless, but about learning from what happened and trying together again.

Not everyone will jump in right away. Sometimes you'll face resistance, maybe someone scoffs at a new ritual or reacts defensively to feedback. Don't take it personally. Change is uncomfortable for most people at first. Stories can help; share an example of a team overcoming conflict by listening better, or tell of a time in your life when better listening resolved something tricky. Stories are less threatening than lectures and help people envision what's possible.

Humor goes a long way, too. Admitting your own listening mistakes, like zoning out or jumping in with advice, shows that you're still improving. This humility makes others feel more comfortable, encouraging them to be honest about their own struggles. People are more willing to learn from someone relatable than from a know-it-all.

The best way to gain buy-in is to let others join the process, rather than dictating new rules. Try, "I'm working on being a better listener. Does anyone want to join me?" Or ask, "What would make our meetings more focused?" "How can we be sure everyone gets heard at dinner?" When people help create new rituals or customs, they feel more invested in them.

Expect some efforts to feel awkward or even flop at first, maybe a check-in feels forced, or someone ignores the ground rules. That's normal; change is messy. If something doesn't work, laugh it off and adjust. Treat every attempt as practice, not as a test you pass or fail.

Small wins will start to appear; a normally quiet person might share more, or your teen might linger after dinner because they feel heard. Celebrate these: "I loved how everyone waited their turn tonight." "It was great hearing different perspectives in our meeting." Acknowledging these moments shows everyone that listening really does make a difference.

Setbacks happen; if someone slips into interrupting or dominating, gently redirect: "Let's make sure we all get a turn." Or share your own slip-up: "I caught myself jumping in too soon; let's slow down." Admitting your mistakes keeps things light and makes imperfection normal.

Little by little, these small actions create a bigger shift, growing a culture where listening is valued not just as a skill, but as part of who you are together. You'll notice less tension, more trust, quieter voices speaking up, and fewer heated disagreements because everyone feels safer sharing what's really on their mind.

Remember: inspiring others isn't about being perfect or always right, but about showing up with openness and curiosity, and making room for others to do the same.

Listening Champions Check

Ready to help your team, family, or group listen better? Here's a list to get started:

- Model undivided attention when you can.

- Suggest a listening activity at meetings or meals.

- Begin meetings with appreciations or check-ins.

- Set "one person speaks at a time" ground rules.

- Try listening circles with groups.

- Give positive feedback to good listeners.

- Facilitate group reflection after projects or tough talks.

- Share stories of positive change, your own or others'.

- Use humor and humility about missteps.

- Invite everyone to suggest and create new listening habits.

You don't have to do it all; pick one or two steps and see what shifts.

Building new listening habits is crucial, but helping those around you grow makes an even bigger impact. With patience, example, and creativity, you can plant the seeds for trust and collaboration that last long after today's conversation. Next, we'll explore ways to keep this listening culture strong as life changes, helping you stay connected wherever you go.

Conclusion

Thanks for reading. In our fast-paced world, listening is a powerful skill. I wanted to show you how it helps you cut through the noise, build trust, and connect with others, leading to stronger, more meaningful relationships. Listening really does make a difference.

Listening isn't just for therapists or so-called 'people persons.' It's a practical skill anyone can get better at, which can boost your confidence. When you truly listen, relationships change, teams become more open, stress goes down, and people feel noticed. These small but meaningful changes are the real magic of listening; they can transform things, and anyone can learn them.

Let's look back at what we've covered. You've learned to notice your own listening blind spots, like zoning out, jumping in with advice, or getting defensive when things get emotional. You've seen how active listening works, being present, paraphrasing naturally, asking clear questions, and giving people room to speak. We also talked about empathy, not just the comforting kind, but the everyday skill you can build and protect with good boundaries.

We also tackled the tough parts. Now you have the tools to deal with your own distractions, assumptions, and biases that can block effective listening. You know how to read nonverbal cues, even on video calls, handle tricky cross-cultural situations, and manage those intense conversations that get your heart racing. We even looked at how to listen better in digital spaces, like text messages, group chats, and work apps, so you can keep real connections even when life is busy.

Change happens when you take action. With your toolkit, power pause, paraphrasing, clarifying questions, validation, holding space, micro-habits, reflective tracking, and rituals, start today. Small steps add up to real progress.

Remember this if you slip up or feel like you're starting over: you don't have to be perfect. No one listens perfectly all the time. What matters is making progress and staying committed. Every time you pause before interrupting, pay attention, or say, "I want to make sure I understand," that's a win worth celebrating and keeps you moving forward.

Think of one time when your listening really made a difference. Maybe a friend opened up to you, and you just listened instead of trying to fix things. Maybe the meeting went better because you drew attention to someone's idea that was overlooked. Maybe your partner or child shared more because you let them finish, even if you disagreed. These moments matter. They build trust and connection, and show that your effort is working.

Maybe you feel tired. Maybe you've tried to listen better before, but it didn't last. Maybe people still talk over each other or look at their phones during dinner. Don't let that stop you. Even small changes in how you listen can have effects you might not notice right away. You can't control others, but you can show what real, kind, and intentional listening looks like. That's how change begins.

Here's my challenge for you: pick one tool and use it today. Then ask yourself, "What changed?" Notice your effort, learn from it, and try again. Progress is what matters.

Don't keep this to yourself. The world needs more people who truly listen. Teach what you're learning, show it at work or at home, and share your favorite exercises. Suggest a listening ritual at your next team meeting or family dinner. You might be surprised at how quickly others follow your lead.

Imagine what could change if just 10% more people in your life listened with real intention. There would be less tension, more honest feedback, better teamwork, and much more trust wherever you go. This isn't just wishful thinking. It's a real possibility when more of us choose to listen and truly mean it, making a difference in our communities and beyond.

You're now part of something bigger. Make your next conversation count by listening with intention and creating real change.

A Personal Request from the Author

Thank you for reading *The Power of Truly Listening*.

If this book helped you become more present, ask better questions, understand others more deeply, or handle difficult conversations with greater patience and confidence, I am sincerely grateful.

So many people are longing to be heard, at home, at work, in friendships, on teams, and even in digital conversations. Yet many of them may not realize that better listening is a skill they can learn, practice, and use to build stronger trust and a deeper connection. More people may benefit from the information in this book, but they may never discover it without your help.

If you found this book worthwhile and informative, please consider leaving an honest review. Your review can help another reader recognize the value of this resource and take the first step toward listening with more intention, communicating with more empathy, and building healthier relationships in every area of life.

Your review does not need to be long. A few honest sentences about what helped you most can make a meaningful difference.

Thank you for your support, your time, and your willingness to help this message reach the people who need it most.

With appreciation,
George Munson

Acknowledgements

Beohm, R., & Beohm, R. (2026, April 14). *How to avoid an emotional hijacking | Rachel Beohm*. Rachel Beohm | Writer, Speaker, Coach. https://www.rachelbeohm.com/how-to-avoid-an-emotional-hijacking/

Bergan, J. (2020, June 26). *Holding space during facilitation for difficult conversations*. Youth MOVE National. https://youthmovenational.org/holding-space-during-facilitation-for-diff icult-conversations/

(c) Copyright skillsyouneed.com 2011-2026. (n.d.). *Listening Myths and Misconceptions | SkillsYouNeed*. https://www.skillsyouneed.com/ips/listening-misconceptions.html

Checking your browser - reCAPTCHA. (n.d.). https://pmc.ncbi.nlm.nih.gov/articles/PMC4937233/

Clear, J. (2020, February 4). *Habit Stacking: How to build new habits by taking advantage of old ones*. James Clear. https://jamesclear.com/habit-stacking

Council, F. C. (2024, August 12). *Take these 13 actionable steps to become a better active listener*. Forbes. https://www.forbes.com/councils/forbescoachescouncil/2019/11/15/ta ke-these-13-actionable-steps-to-become-a-better-active-listener/

Ferguson, J. (2026, February 18). *Listen up! The secret to paying attention and becoming a more inclusive leader*. reworked.co.

https://www.reworked.co/leadership/listen-up-the-secret-to-paying-atte
ntion-and-becoming-a-more-inclusive-leader/

Learn &. (n.d.).
https://mha.ohio.gov/wps/portal/gov/mha/get-help/treatment-services/
documents/understanding-compassion-fatigue

Lpc, L. C. P. (2025, July 5). *30 Best journaling
Prompts for improving Mental Health.* PositivePsychology.com.
https://positivepsychology.com/journaling-prompts/

*Making an effective apology | practice |
Greater Good in action.* (2023, December 10).
https://ggia.berkeley.edu/practice/making_an_effective_apology

Mindtools Membership. (2026, January 13).
How good are your listening skills?
https://www.mindtools.com/ai4ff5e/how-good-are-your-listening-skills

O'Donovan, R., & McAuliffe, E. (2020). Exploring psychological safety in
healthcare teams to inform the development of interventions: combining
observational, survey and interview data. *BMC Health Services Research,
20*(1), 810. https://doi.org/10.1186/s12913-020-05646-z

Pearn Kandola. (2026, January 5). *Inclusive team communication:
Bridging differences effectively.*
https://pearnkandola.com/insights/inclusive-team-communication-brid
ging-differences-effectively/

Rathore, S. (2022, July 5). *How to lead
better virtual meetings.* Harvard Business Review.
https://hbr.org/2022/07/how-to-lead-better-virtual-meetings

Rawlings, A. (2022, February 24). *Why emoji mean different things in
different cultures.*
https://www.bbc.com/future/article/20181211-why-emoji-mean-differe
nt-things-in-different-cultures

Segal, J., PhD, Smith, M., MA, Robinson, L., Boose, G., Segal, J., PhD, Smith, M., MA, Robinson, L., & Boose, G. (2026, February 4). Body language and nonverbal communication. *HelpGuide.org*. https://www.helpguide.org/relationships/communication/nonverbal -communication

Shoshan, H. N., & Wehrt, W. (2025). "Zoom fatigue" revisited: Are video meetings still exhausting post-COVID-19? *Journal of Occupational Health Psychology, 30*(5), 353–364. https://doi.org/10.1037/ocp0000409

Smith, A. (2023, September 16). *37 Validating Statements (A quick cheat sheet for when you are stuck) — Amanda L. Smith, LCSW*. Amanda L. Smith, LCSW. https://www.hopeforbpd.com/borderline-personality-disorder-treat ment/validating-statements

Stop the meeting madness. (2017, July 1). Harvard Business Review. https://hbr.org/2017/07/stop-the-meeting-madness

Tennant, K., Long, A., & Toney-Butler, T. J. (2023, September 13). *Active listening*. StatPearls - NCBI Bookshelf. https://www.ncbi.nlm.nih.gov/books/NBK442015/

The Listening Crisis: How extractive Habits are Reshaping communication - Frank Hawkins Kenan Institute of Private Enterprise. (n.d.). Frank Hawkins Kenan Institute of Private Enterprise. https://kenaninstitute.unc.edu/kenan-insight/the-listening-crisis-ho w-extractive-habits-are-reshaping-communication/

Thompson, B. S. a. H. (2024, February 20). Now hear this! Most people stink at listening [Excerpt]. *Scientific American*. https://www.scientificamerican.com/article/plateau-effect-digital-gad get-distraction-attention/

Toegel, G., & Barsoux, J. (2016, June 8). *3 situations where Cross-Cultural communication breaks down*. Harvard Business Review.

https://hbr.org/2016/06/3-situations-where-cross-cultural-communication-breaks-down

Travers, M. (2025, April 26). *5 'Micro-Moments' that slowly end your relationship, by a psychologist.* Forbes. https://www.forbes.com/sites/traversmark/2025/04/26/5-micro-moments-that-slowly-end-your-relationship-by-a-psychologist/

Wignall, N. (2025, January 12). *How to Take Feedback without Getting Defensive.* Nick Wignall. https://nickwignall.com/how-to-take-feedback-without-getting-defensive/